BIZARRE LONDON

DISCOVER THE CAPITAL'S SECRETS & SURPRISES

DAVID LONG

Skyhorse Publishing
A Herman Graf book

First published in the United Kingdom
by Constable, an imprint of Little, Brown Book Group.

This edition published by Skyhorse, 2019

Skyhorse publishing books may be purchased in bulk at special discounts for sales promotion, corporate gifts, fund-raising, or educational purposes. Special editions can also be created to specifications. For details, contact the Special Sales Department, Skyhorse Publishing, 307 West 36th Street, 11th Floor, New York, New York 10018 or info@skyhorsepublishing.com

www.skyhorsepublishing.com

10 9 8 7 6 5 4 3 2

Library of Congress Cataloging-in-Publication Data available on file

Cover design by Daniel Brount
Cover illustrations: iStockphoto

Print ISBN: 978-1-5107-4211-6
Ebook ISBN: 978-1-6287-3925-1

Printed in China

Contents

Introduction

As a sprawling world city covering some 600 square miles, with 300 different languages spoken and more than 8 million people sharing a history stretching back 2,000 years, it's hardly surprising that London throws up so much that is strange, unexplained or just plain odd.

From a highwayman dressed as a bishop to a duke so shy he surrounded his garden with frosted glass walls nearly 80 ft tall, it's always had more than its fair share of eccentrics. Londoners have similarly been subject to some of the weirdest laws, requiring golfers to wear red, MPs not to wear armour, and the rest of us to abstain from carrying planks along pavements or playing cards within a mile of an arsenal or explosives store.

And, of course, London has also been able to lay claim to some of the most extraordinary buildings anywhere in Britain. From an underground café converted from a council loo to an authentic Tudor palace moved brick by brick to a more attractive riverside setting, they include Britain's tallest family home – spread over eleven floors of a genuine Wren church spire – as well as its smallest listed building and a museum of anaesthetics.

But even so, in a place like London – not that anywhere is remotely like London – this sort of thing is only the start. Britain's shortest canal, its least secret 'secret' bunker and most private public house, its biggest bang, the only part of the National Cycle Network on which bikes are banned, and the most outrageously expensive takeaway meal ever ordered – you'll find them all in the following pages.

From Boudicca to Boris and beyond, the list of curiosities is as long as it is varied. Skating on lard? The Victorians were doing it in London. Sixty days of rioting after theatre prices went up by sixpence? That happened here, too, in 1809. And the world's first ever female urinal? Well, that made its debut in London in the 1920s, but had to be removed almost immediately when women started using it in 'an uncleanly manner'. How could anyone be tired of London?

David Long, May 2013
www.davidlong.info

I

Gruesome London

'And in any case, I have only a little neck.'

Anne Boleyn

Exceptional Executions

1531 – Richard Rouse

Rouse met an appropriate end for a cook. Found guilty of attempting to poison his master, he was boiled alive on a spot between Bart's Hospital and Smithfield's meat market. The meal he had prepared made the Bishop of Rochester deeply unwell, and sixteen of his attendants died. After being briefly displayed on a spike, Rouse's head was chucked into the river.

1541 – Countess of Salisbury

The last direct descendant of the Plantagenet line, the Countess was doomed after appearing to side with Catherine of Aragon against Henry VIII. On the day – small, frail, ill and sixty-eight years old – she refused to submit to the block and had to be forced down on to it. As she struggled, the axe struck her a glancing blow on the shoulder but somehow she leapt up and attempted to run for it. Once subdued, it took another ten blows to finish the old lady off.

1666 – Robert Hubert

The French watchmaker was hanged after admitting he started the Great Fire of London. In reality, he had been framed for the crime by anti-Catholics, but burning down a house carried the death penalty at the time. Londoners wanted revenge for the more than 13,000 properties that had been lost to the flames, and Hubert – Catholic, foreign, apparently stealing highly paid work from English craftsmen – was in the wrong place at the wrong time, and must have fitted the bill perfectly.

1685 – The Duke of Monmouth

The illegitimate son of Charles II, when the Duke of Monmouth was found guilty of treason in 1685, the inept executioner, Jack Ketch, took five blows with an axe. Even then, as he was almost certainly drunk, his work had to be finished off by a man with a knife.

1689 – Patrick O'Bryan

Primitive technology has enabled the odd villain to escape the drop, but it's a myth that if the mechanism failed they were declared free men. O'Bryan was a convicted footpad – a thief who preyed on pedestrians – who somehow survived a hanging. But when he was re-caught, re-convicted and re-hanged, his body was then boiled in tar to make absolutely sure he wouldn't escape justice again.

THE ETIQUETTE OF EXECUTION

Until 1753, women found guilty of murdering their husbands could expect to be burned at the stake, although kindly attempts were sometimes made to strangle them before the flames really began to hurt. For centuries, beheading was similarly considered more honourable than hanging, and the really privileged – such as Anne Boleyn, as queen – might be dispatched with a sword rather than the more mundane and brutal axe.

Hanging was always thought good enough for the masses, however, and traditionally condemned men (and not a few women) were taken from Newgate Gaol in the walled city – where the Old Bailey is today – to the so-called Tyburn Tree north of Hyde Park. On the way, each would be presented with scented nosegays by crowds that could number into the tens of thousands. Convicts could also enjoy a last drink free of charge along the way.

The pub of choice was the Mason's Arms, which is still open for business today in Seymour Place, W1. There is nothing left of the gallows, however, which stood in what is now the south-west corner of Connaught Square. The structure was large enough to hang twenty-one at a time and, bizarrely, there was an order in which the executions were to be carried out. Traditionally, the public liked to see highwaymen dispatched first – as the so-called 'aristocrats of crime' (see Chapter 17) – then common thieves, and finally anyone convicted of treason.

1701 – 'Captain' William Kidd

The Scots sailor-turned-pirate was probably no worse than any other but he has somehow become legend. As befits his trade, he was hanged on the Thames at Wapping Stairs, for long enough for three tides to wash over his body, and then again at Tilbury where his rotting corpse was left swinging in the wind for more than twenty years.

1811 – John Williams

Accused of the hideous Ratcliffe Highway Murders – when members of two families had their throats cut – Williams was, in all likelihood, innocent, but hanged himself in his cell before a jury could decide. With suicide illegal, and (more significantly) bloodthirsty Londoners feeling cheated of the gruesome spectacle they felt they deserved, his corpse was paraded through East London and a stake driven through his heart before the burial at the crossroads of New Road and Cannon Street Road, E1.

1817 – John Cashman

After robbing a gunsmith's on Snow Hill, and injuring one of the shop assistants, Cashman was convicted and, unsurprisingly, sentenced to death. He was then taken back to the shop and hanged outside it, the last time in London a criminal was sentenced to die at the scene of his crime.

1824 – Henry Fauntleroy

Estimated to have been the largest crowd ever assembled anywhere in Britain for a public execution, at least 100,000 Londoners are thought to have gathered outside Newgate Gaol to see banker Henry Fauntleroy hang. His crime was defrauding the Bank of England of £250,000 and wasting nearly the whole lot.

1868 – Michael Barrett

A member of the Fenians – the Irish brotherhood dedicated to freedom from British rule – Barrett was the last man to be publicly hanged in England after putting a bomb in a wheelbarrow against the outer wall of Clerkenwell's House of Detention (see Chapter 16). His intention had been to help prisoners to escape, but instead the blast killed twelve and injured more than a hundred others.

For what became known as the Clerkenwell Outrage, he was hanged outside Newgate Gaol. The occasion proved to be one of those strange meeting places of old and new, with crowds arriving at Farringdon on the newfangled Underground railway to witness an event that was positively medieval. Barrett's body was interred within the prison walls and then, in 1903, taken to the City of London Cemetery in Newham and reburied.

1961 – Edwin Bush

The twenty-one-year-old murderer – the first to be caught using Identikit pictures – was also the last person to be hanged at Pentonville Prison. This had become Britain's own 'death row' in 1902 when the dreaded Newgate Gaol closed, and more people were hanged here during the twentieth century than at any other British prison. The total included 109 murderers, 6 spies and 2 traitors.

THE GREAT WEN'S WICKEDEST WOMEN

According to the radical pamphleteer William Cobbett in his 1830 work *Rural Rides*, London's rapid growth as a major city was more like a pathological swelling on the face of the nation. In other words, it was a 'wen', or a pus-filled boil. And there have been a number of notably wicked women over the years who are now inextricably linked with the Great Wen's darker moments:

Elizabeth Brownrigg (1720–67)

A midwife in the City of London, Brownrigg employed young girls to help her in her work and was hanged at Tyburn when the extent of the sadistic treatment meted out to her innocent charges became known. One in particular, sixteen-year-old Mary Clifford, was reportedly chained, naked, to an outhouse door. Sleeping on straw in a coal-hole, Clifford had earlier been suspended from a beam, stripped and horsewhipped until covered in blood or her tormentor became too tired to continue. She died of her injuries.

Following a public hanging and dissection, Brownrigg's skeleton was put on display in a specially constructed niche in the wall of the Royal College of Surgeons.

Amelia Dyer (1838–96)

The most prolific baby-murderer of the Victorian age, Dyer trained as a nurse and, for more than twenty years, plied her trade as a so-called baby farmer. Taking newborns from those who didn't want them, she would charge a fee for bringing them up herself or finding them new homes.

Dyer quickly realised that killing them was quicker, easier and more profitable, and while the precise number of her victims will never be known, it is thought to run as high as 300. When the body of one washed up in the Thames, she was sent for trial and was hanged at Newgate Gaol.

Isabella of France (1295–1358)

The reviled 'She-wolf of France', Isabella was the Queen Consort of Edward II of England and mother to Edward III. She was also the lover of Roger de Mortimer, Earl of March, and conspired with him to steal the throne and rule the country through her young, weak son.

Imprisoning her husband at Berkeley Castle in 1327, Isabella had him murdered with a 'horn or funnel ... thrust into his fundament through which a red-hot spit was run up his bowels'. Buried in Grey Friar's Monastery, Newgate, her beautiful ghost is said still to flit through the churchyard clutching her husband's heart to her breast.

Bloody Mary (1516–58)

The only surviving child of Henry VIII and Catherine of Aragon, during her five-year reign Mary I sought violently to return the English to Catholicism. To this end, she ordered or allowed the torture and execution of prominent Protestants, hundreds of whom were burned at the stake.

As many as 800 fled the country to escape the ferocity of the so-called Marian Persecutions, but an estimated 284 died. Mary was subsequently vilified in (John) *Foxe's Book of Martyrs* although, in reality, dying without issue, she was no worse than her successor, Elizabeth I, who showed no mercy to Catholic dissenters.

Marguerite Fahmy (1890–1971)

Despite confessing to having shot her husband at the Savoy Hotel in 1923, the wife of the late Prince Ali Kamel Fahmy Bey escaped conviction even for manslaughter. She did so after a bravura performance by her barrister, who quite openly appealed to the all-white jury's solidly racist instincts.

'I ask you,' said Sir Edward Marshall Hall KC, addressing the jury, 'to open the gate and let this western woman go back into the light of God's great western sun.' To the fury of the Egyptian Embassy, they did so, acquitting Sir Edward's client and allowing Madame Fahmy to walk free.

Toffs with Blood on Their Hands

Lord Lucan

Dead or alive, and still very much Britain's most famous fugitive, Richard John Bingham, 7th Earl of Lucan, went on the run in November 1974 and cannot reliably be said to have been seen since. The peer fled after murdering the nanny at his Belgravia home, perhaps mistaking her for his wife.

After a bloodstained car was found at Newhaven, it seemed most likely that the Earl had fled across the Channel – or possibly thrown himself into it, although the evidence of a body to confirm this theory has never been found. Rumours persist that he was helped to escape by rich and influential friends, and sightings continue to be reported in the tabloids with predictable regularity.

Laurence Shirly, 4th Earl Ferrers

Even in death, peers are traditionally said to enjoy special privileges, the best known being the right to be hanged with a silken cord. The last member of the House of Lords to be hanged was dispatched in 1760, but there is alas no evidence to suggest Lord Ferrers dangled at the end of anything but an ordinary rope of common hemp.

Earlier that year, his lordship had been visited by a servant to discuss rents on the family estate at Staunton Harold, Leicestershire. Lord Ferrers shot him dead and, reflecting on the huge crowds at Tyburn, his prophetic last words were: 'I suppose they never saw a lord hanged, and perhaps they will never see another.'

Sir Ralph de Standish

In June 1341, when revolting peasants marched on London from Essex and Kent, talks were arranged at Smithfield between

Richard II and the peasant's leader, Wat Tyler. Things went quickly awry, however, with the Lord Mayor, William Walworth, drawing his dagger and wounding Tyler in the neck.

Seeking to defend the King – Richard was still a boy of fourteen – de Standish, one of his squires, quickly moved in. He stabbed Tyler to death with a short sword, hence it is said the event is represented in the red of a blade in the City arms today. He was shortly afterwards knighted for his prompt action.

Baron Dacre

Thomas Fiennes, 9th Lord Dacre, inherited his grandfather's title and Herstmonceux Castle in Sussex and was a member of the jury at the trial of Anne Boleyn. In 1541, in the company of friends, he went poaching and was arrested after an affray that left John Busbrig fatally wounded.

Dacre and his pals were charged with murder, his Lordship being persuaded to plead guilty and throw himself on the mercy of the King. He did so, but the sovereign's mercy only went so far. While his co-accused were beheaded, he was taken to Tyburn and, according to a witness, 'strangled as common murderers are'.

HRH Albert Victor Christian Edward

George V's older brother (known as 'Eddy') was certainly a bit of a royal wrong'un, but his guilt is far from proven. Since the 1960s, however, his name has frequently been mentioned as a possible candidate for Jack the Ripper, the suggestion being that he was driven to kill after going mad as a consequence of contracting syphilis.

More recently it has been suggested that Eddy killed in order to conceal an illegal marriage to a Catholic commoner with whom he'd had a son. In truth, HRH had some very robust alibis, and the story is nonsense, but this has not prevented the sputtering flames of suspicion being kept alive by enthusiastic if ill-informed Ripperologists and the occasional republican.

Lord George Gordon

The twenty-nine-year-old duke's son was probably only indirectly responsible for the many hundreds of deaths that occurred during the 1780 anti-Catholic riots that bore his name (see Chapter 17). As their instigator, he did well to escape being found guilty of high treason, especially as nearly thirty of his supporters were sentenced to death.

Admittedly, he spent eight months in the Tower of London, but he was then set free on the grounds that he had merely lost control of the mob rather than egging them on. While incarcerated, he was also allowed an unusual degree of luxury – for example, he frequently entertained guests to dinner in his cell – and on his release he moved to the Midlands, converted to Judaism and changed his name to 'Yisrael bar Avraham' ('Israel Son of Abraham').

SO MUCH FOR THE GOOD OLD DAYS

In London, the application of the death penalty reached its zenith during the elegant Georgian period, when the number of capital offences increased to well over 200. It is hard not to see the escalation as just a cynical ploy to cut the cost of imprisoning offenders for long periods, and, for a while, citizens of London could be hanged for such trivial crimes as the theft of five shillings (the equivalent of 25p today) or impersonating a Chelsea Pensioner. Consequently, between 1770 and 1830, as many as 35,000 death sentences are thought to have been handed down.

Ten London Serial Killers

Dennis Nilsen – fifteen victims

Immortalised as the 'Muswell Hill Murderer' (and more rarely as the 'Cricklewood Killer'), Nilsen murdered fifteen young men in north London, dissecting them and retaining some parts while flushing others down the loo. He was convicted in 1983 when the drains at his home became blocked by the sheer quantity of organic matter Nilsen had forced into the system.

John Haigh – nine victims

The notorious 'Acid Bath Murderer' was hanged in 1949 after using a vat of corrosive liquid to conceal his crimes. In the mistaken belief that there could be no conviction without a body, Haigh was undone through some brilliant forensic work by a Home Office pathologist who found traces of human fat in amongst the congealing gloop . . . and some acid-proof false teeth. In the hope that he would be deemed insane and escape with his life, Haigh insisted he was a vampire – but this ruse failed.

Jack the Stripper – eight victims

In the mid-1960s, a mystery killer in west London got away with murdering six working girls, with another two probable victims. Their bodies, strangled and stripped, were dumped in or near the Thames at Hammersmith and, despite interviewing an incredible 7,000 witnesses, police were never able to nail anyone for the crimes. World Champion boxer Freddie Mills remains a leading suspect, but he killed himself in Soho before it could be proved either way.

John Childs – six victims

A contract killer who killed six people for cash, Childs attempted to incinerate the evidence in the fireplace of his Poplar flat after dismembering the bodies. He was sent down in 1980, the *Independent* newspaper describing how, for at least two of the murders, Childs had dressed all in black – complete with an undertaker's top hat – to heighten the dramatic effect of his sickening crimes.

Jack the Ripper – five victims

Victorian London's most famous killer has spawned more books, plays and movies than any other, with an estimated 100 names in the frame for who might actually have killed the women. Perhaps the most extraordinary thing is how he got away with it – that he was a man is one of very few things Ripperologists can agree on – and that, unlike every other serial killer, he brought his activities to an end without first being caught.

Robert Maudsley – four victims

After working as a rent boy in the London of the Swinging Sixties, Maudsley killed a man with a hammer and was sent to Broadmoor. Since his incarceration, he killed three more times, and is now one of an estimated three dozen British serial killers whose so-called whole life tariffs mean they will never be released.

Gordon Cummins – four victims

Six attacks in six days, and four of them fatal, the 'Blackout Ripper' took full advantage of wartime lighting regulations to conceal his vicious assaults on women in the West End in 1942. Fortunately, he dropped a gas mask case near the scene of one of his attacks and was traced using his RAF personnel number. The twenty-eight-year-old was strung up after the briefest of trials and, with a war still to win, there was minimal press coverage. This is probably why these days he has been more or less forgotten.

Thomas Wainewright – four victims

In it for the money, in 1830 Wainewright insured his sister-in-law for an astonishing £18,000 (£15 million today) and then bumped her off. He fled to France but, on his return years later, was suspected of killing his uncle, his mother-in-law and a friend. Lacking firm proof after so long, the authorities charged him with fraud instead, but after being transported to Tasmania he confessed to what he had done.

George Chapman – three victims

Arrested in 1902 for the murder of three barmaids, two of whom he claimed to have married, Chapman's notoriety was assured when a policeman joked about having caught Jack the Ripper. In reality, the preferences of the two killers were completely different – poison versus mutilation, barmaids versus prostitutes – but Ripper fever has never abated, and the public likes nothing more than a new suspect to theorise about.

John Straffen – three victims

Initially incarcerated at Wandsworth, Straffen was locked up for a total of fifty-five years, which still stands as a UK record. In 1951, the twenty-one-year-old killed two young girls, and then a third after escaping from Broadmoor, and he died in 1977 without ever being released. At the time of his conviction, Straffen was diagnosed as a 'major mental defective' and is now thought to have had an IQ of just 58.

HEADS YOU LOSE

Simon of Sudbury's head was hacked off during the Peasants' Revolt of 1381 after the Archbishop of Canterbury, Richard II's hated Chancellor, had been dragged out of the Tower of London where he had taken refuge. His head is now preserved in a church in his Suffolk home town.

In 1661, on the twelfth anniversary of Charles I's murder, Oliver Cromwell's corpse was dug up and ritually beheaded. His putrefying bonce spent some years on a pike outside Westminster Hall, and it was to be nearly 300 years before it was finally reburied, at Sidney Sussex College, Cambridge, his *alma mater.*

The head of the wooden effigy of Edward III in Westminster Abbey is a rare example of medieval realism. It shows the king's mouth drooping to the left, presumably a symptom of the stroke that killed him, a surprising feature from an era when rulers were traditionally depicted in an idealised form.

With a minimum of ceremony, and in the absence of a coffin, Anne Boleyn's neatly excised head was crammed into an arrow box alongside her body. This was then buried beneath the floor of the church of St Peter ad Vincula in the Tower of London, and remained there undisturbed until the 1870s.

After his bungled beheading in 1685, the two halves of the Duke of Monmouth are popularly supposed to have been sewn back together in order that the dead duke could 'sit' for a family portrait.

In 1305, the head of William Wallace was parboiled and dipped in pitch to preserve it and then displayed on London Bridge. The tradition of doing this to traitors continued until 1660 and is commemorated today by a white spike at the southern end of the bridge's modern replacement, after the original London Bridge was relocated in 1967 in its entirety to Lake Havasu City, Arizona, USA. The new spike is enormous, but hardly anyone seems to notice it or know what it symbolises.

2

Ghostly London

In the days and weeks following 10 October 1971, when the old London Bridge officially reopened following its stone-by-stone removal to Lake Havasu City in Arizona, reports began of figures in Victorian dress being seen strolling around the local scrublands. It's a nice idea, and the logic of it is irresistible, but in general the ghosts of London tend to stay put, and do so in sufficient numbers to give the capital a reputation as one of the most haunted places on the planet.

Perhaps given its long and eventful past, that's hardly surprising. A history steeped in legend, the survival of literally thousands of historic buildings – not to mention a network of narrow streets and alleys in the Square Mile[1] that have somehow resisted the developers – it's no wonder that ghost-hunters have found the capital to be home to so many spirits, and from so many different centuries and walks of life.

1 Which, incidentally, and somewhat irritatingly, is these days a messy and imperfect 1.16 square miles following boundary changes in the 1990s that incorporated an area north of London Wall into the City of London.

Indeed, whether you choose to follow in the footsteps of Jack the Ripper – who is said to leap from Westminster Bridge as Big Ben sounds each New Year's Eve – to explore some of the quieter corners of the ancient City of London, or to spend time in the crypts and cloisters of St Paul's and Westminster Abbey, you'll soon hear about – or experience for yourself – something to make your spine tingle.

Not all the ghosts are quite as old as you might suppose, however. In Westminster Abbey, for example, it is said that after the crowds have dispersed on Armistice Day, a uniformed figure has been observed to materialise by the Tomb of the Unknown Soldier. A moving spectacle, his head bowed in sorrow at his own fate and that of his dead comrades, it must be a chilling sight.

Stories about most London spirits, though, tend to concentrate on the departed of earlier eras, and by quite a margin. Still at the Abbey, for example, there is the floating medieval monk known as Father Benedictus who reportedly hovers a foot or two above the floor of the Abbey. Most commonly seen between 5.00 and 6.00 p.m. in and around the cloister, he has been known to engage visitors in conversation, many of whom (including a celebrated couple of Americans in the 1930s) don't seem to realise that they are talking to a ghost.

The legendary 'Princes in the Tower' are also said to haunt the Abbey from time to time, having been buried there when their bodies were rediscovered in 1674. That said, and for understandable reasons, their two ghosts (still holding on to each other, and crying in terror) have more often been seen to materialise in various rooms of the Tower of London, the place where they are thought to have been confined by their uncle, the much-maligned King Richard III.

The Tower, predictably, is one of the ghost-hunter's richest grounds – as well it might be after nearly 1,000 years. As long ago as the thirteenth century, labourers working there claimed that the ghost of St Thomas à Becket had twice destroyed their work with a sweep of his crozier. And each year on 21 May, the ghost of the hapless Henry VI is said to pace up and down the Wakefield Tower marking the anniversary of his murder.

But perhaps the most unnerving is the murmuring and mysterious yellow glow that has been reported in the nearby Salt Tower. Accompanied by a touch 'like cold fingers on the back of the neck' say those who have witnessed it, this strange phenomenon has been attributed to Henry Walpole, a Jesuit who was viciously tortured here on the orders of Henry VIII.

Naturally, the Tower has its very own 'white lady', too, as well as a mysterious, shimmering phial of bluey-white liquid that flies through one of the ancient windows, and the floating, evanescent figures of at least two ill-fated queens. These are, of course, Lady Jane Grey and Anne Boleyn, each of whom came to a famously bloody end on the premises. The ghost of the last-named was once even challenged by a sentry, who reportedly fainted when she ran on to his bayonet and straight through him. Later court-martialled for falling asleep on duty (a technical desertion in military law), he was acquitted on the evidence of two bystanders who said they had witnessed the whole extraordinary episode.

Somewhat less expected, perhaps, is the sighting of a ghost on the London Underground, although having cut a swathe through scores of ancient grave sites, beneath countless churchyards and more than its fair share of plague pits, it is maybe not that surprising that mysterious presences have occasionally been detected in more than a few of the network's tunnels and stations.

Not far from the Tower, for example, station staff at Aldgate have been keeping a log of haunting incidents since the 1950s. In one of them, a maintenance worker is said to have survived an incredible 22,000-volt shock from the third rail, and to have done so immediately after a colleague had observed what he took to be a grey-haired figure – his guardian angel, perhaps? – stroking the man's hair.

50 Berkeley Square: London's Most Haunted House?

For more than seventy years, the beautifully preserved William Kent townhouse, premises of leading antiquarian booksellers Maggs Bros, on the west side of Mayfair's Berkeley Square, have long enjoyed a reputation as the capital's most ghost-infested private home.

During his tenancy of the building, Prime Minister George Canning (1770–1827) was among the first to witness strange goings-on in the house and, at various times, there have been reports of a malevolent brown 'mist' on the staircase, as well as a ghostly white figure – possibly a young woman who jumped to her death from the attic after being propositioned by an older man. Add to this stories of young blades accepting a bet to spend a night in the house but then being carried out dead or insensible the following morning.

In the way of these things, details are sketchy to say the least, but the house was certainly occupied several times by the sort of colourful characters who, we like to think, might leave behind traces of their presence. Besides the Prime Minister, these included a reclusive nonagenarian called Miss Curzon for much of the early eighteenth century, a man called Myers who rarely stepped out in public after being jilted by his fiancée, and a lunatic who was locked away in an upstairs room by his brother.

As for the gamblers, only Lord Lyttelton of Frankley (1744–79) is said to have escaped unaffected. He was armed with a blunderbuss, which he claimed he used to shoot at an apparition. A few weeks later, he said he dreamed of a lady in white who told him he had three days to live . . . and three days later he died aged just thirty-five.

At Bethnal Green Tube station, in 1981, a member of staff claimed to have heard the sound of children crying, an echo, it is thought, of more than 170 local residents who died at the station during the Second World War. (During a panic, hundreds of them sought shelter from incoming enemy bombers, and many were crushed in the stampede.) Covent Garden is similarly said to be haunted by the ghost of the successful actor-manager William Terriss, who was stabbed to death outside the stage door of the Adelphi Theatre in Maiden Lane in 1897. Across the river at Elephant and Castle, the ghost of a young woman has similarly been seen to pass through the carriages and down one of the tunnels.

Back above ground, in 1982, another equally mysterious figure made herself known when a photographer visited the glorious eighteenth-century interior of St Botolph-without-Bishopsgate on the edge of the City. Developing his film a few hours later, Chris Brackley found that in one picture the apparition could be seen gazing down at him from the gallery. Surprised, as he knew the only other person in the building at the time was his wife, Brackley was later contacted by a builder who, working in the crypt a while previously, claimed to have dislodged the lid of a coffin revealing the well-preserved face of a woman whose description closely matched that of the pale figure in the photograph.

Still in the City, the magnificent precincts of the Old Lady of Threadneedle Street, the Bank of England, are haunted by another lady of their own. Dressed in black mourning clothes and nicknamed 'the Bank Nun', she is thought to be the spirit of Sarah Whitehead whose brother Phillip was found guilty of forgery and executed in 1812. Presumably following a breakdown, Sarah refused to acknowledge what had happened and became a regular visitor to the bank in the years before her own death. Typically, she would call in to the bank several times a week, on each occasion collaring staff members and demanding of them, 'Have you seen my brother?'

Her story is sad but not as chilling as the screams frequently heard around the medieval gatehouse of St Bartholomew the Great – restored by Sir Aston Webb, architect of Buckingham Palace's most familiar façade – or the story of a curse that is said to hover over the British Museum. There, the decorated sarcophagi and skeletal remains of the mummies make the first-floor Egyptian Galleries some of the most visited rooms in the museum, and also the most haunted.

One of the exhibits in particular, a mummy labelled only as 'unnamed singer of Amen-Re', is said by believers to have put a curse on all its future keepers. Following its discovery in Egypt in the 1880s, the first person to buy it disappeared without a trace, a second was wounded in a shooting accident, while the third, fearing for his life, hurriedly sold the mummy on to an antiquary. He shipped it to London some time around 1888, but as soon as it was sold, a spiritual medium warned the new owner to get rid of it on pain of death. In pretty short order, it was somehow implicated in the death of a photographer who'd attempted to take a picture of it for an advertisement and then – more bizarrely – in the deaths of all the pets belonging to its final private owner.

Suitably warned, she arranged for the mummy to come to the British Museum, but the curse struck one more time, killing one of the porters carrying the exhibit up to the first floor. Happily, no more has been heard from the anonymous performer since an exorcism was carried out on it by two psychics in 1921.

And finally, after all, it is perhaps this fear of their being exorcised that keeps a few of London's more famous ghosts out in the cold, where maybe they feel safer. How else to explain a spirit matching the description of Lord Nelson, for example, which has been observed crossing the great courtyard at Somerset House? He never enters any of the buildings that once housed the Admiralty, where his brother Maurice Nelson was on the staff. And in St James's Park, witnesses have similarly reported a headless woman rising out of the water before running into the nearby bushes. She is thought by some to be the wife of a guardsman, a maniac who hacked off her head and slipped her body into the lake.

TIME, GENTLEMEN, PLEASE!

The Grenadier's dead subaltern is perhaps London's most famous pub ghost (see Chapter 14), but with so many ancient taverns in the capital it's no surprise that more than a few claim to be haunted:

Ten Bells, Commercial Street, E1

Formerly called 'The Jack the Ripper', as recently as 1996 the pub was said to have been taken over by the ghost of Annie Chapman, one of the Ripper's victims. Poltergeist activity has also been reported, together with 'inexplicable' gusts of wind, none of which can be bad for business.

Flask Tavern, Highgate West Hill, N6

An apparition of a young lady has been seen entering and leaving the pub, and is thought to be the ghost of a barmaid who committed suicide on the premises. (More unusual perhaps is the chicken that is said to haunt nearby Pond Square, possibly the very chicken the philosopher Francis Bacon was stuffing with snow in 1626 – to test its value as a preservative – when he caught a chill and died.)

The Spaniards Inn, Spaniards Road, NW3

The car park is said to be haunted by a horse, and with no credible justification this is said to be Dick Turpin's famous Black Bess. More believable, perhaps, are reports of 'Black

Dick', a seedy moneylender who was knocked down and killed by a coach outside. His ghost is said occasionally to trouble drinkers in the bar by tugging at their clothes.

The Anchor Bankside, Park Street, SE1

This famous riverside pub in Southwark is another where claims of a non-human haunting have often been made, this time with reports of the ghost of a dog, which, in the early eighteenth century, was injured while trying to protect its master from footpads or drunks. A member of the gang is said to have violently slammed a heavy pub door on the dog, severing its tail and sending it scurrying into the night, since when it has never been seen again. Not alive, anyway.

The George, Strand, WC2

A timbered fake, the present 1930s pub replaced one with much earlier origins. This perhaps explains the occasional presence of the ghost of a seventeenth-century Cavalier that is said to haunt the premises. It once surprised a decorator who was whitewashing the cellars. The staff were so used to the manifestation – which, obviously, they call George – that they had not thought to warn him first.

The Viaduct Tavern, Newgate Street, EC1

Wrongly but frequently said to incorporate some of the old Newgate Gaol cells in its cellar – which, sadly but absolutely, do not exist – the City's last remaining Victorian gin palace has a poltergeist. Nicknamed Fred, he slams doors and blows fuses and on at least one occasion in the 1990s removed an entire roll of carpet that two workmen had taken up in order to work on the floorboards.

The Rising Sun, Cloth Fair, EC1

This is one of several pubs close to Bart's Hospital that are said to have been popular with the area's 'resurrection men' or grave robbers. The ghost at the lovely Rising Sun nevertheless sounds like more of a peeping tom than a bodysnatcher. On more than one occasion, it reportedly attempted to remove the bedclothes of two barmaids who lived there during the 1980s, and, more recently, another female member of staff felt an ice-cold hand run down her back while she was taking a shower. Nothing has ever been seen, but footsteps have been heard in the empty bar.

The Bow Bells, Bow Road, E3

Made visible by a gaudy orange frontage, this East End pub has a ghost that is said to haunt the ladies' loo. An attempt was made to flush it out in 1974, despite the fact that reports of ghosts are usually good for business; but during the exorcism, the loo door flew open with such force that the glass was shattered and the proceedings brought to a halt.

The Black Swan, Bow Road, E3

Hit during a Zeppelin raid in the Great War, a number of victims – including the landlord's daughters Cissie and Sylvia – were said to haunt the bar before the rebuilt pub was demolished in the 1970s. Unusually, the high-flying dirigible – no. L-33 – was later brought down near Colchester on 24 September 1916 and the crew taken into custody.

More Modern Manifestations

Historic buildings one somehow expects to be haunted, and most reports of ghosts seem to involve spirits dressed in Victorian clothes or something even earlier. But a death's a death and, if one believes in spirits at all, then surely logic suggests that new buildings – and a few more recent victims – will also get their chance to shine.

Heathrow Airport

On a densely foggy day in March 1948, an incoming Douglas DC3 operated by Sabena crash-landed at the airport, killing all three crew and seventeen of its twenty-two passengers. With visibility down to a couple of hundred yards, rescue workers reported having a conversation with a man who appeared from nowhere asking if anyone had seen his briefcase. Since then, there have been occasional reports of a spectral figure on one of the two runways, a man whose description sounds similar to the strange report on the day of the crash. On at least one occasion, police and a fire truck have been dispatched to an area where the figure had been seen wandering around on the tarmac, but on arrival no trace of anyone has ever been found.

The London Palladium

As theatres go, the Palladium on Argyll Street is a relatively new one, barely a hundred years old despite its neo-classical façade. Nevertheless, and like a number of older theatres (including the Adelphi and Her Majesty's), it is said to be haunted, this time by the ghost of a young woman called either Helen Campbell or Mrs Shireburn who appears on a staircase at the back of the Royal Circle.

Unusually, neither name has any theatrical connection but both are thought to be linked to Argyll House, a large townhouse that formerly occupied the same site. This belonged to a Scottish nobleman – Archibald Campbell, 3rd Duke of Argyll (1682–1761).

Broadcasting House

The BBC's iconic headquarters was completed in 1934, but is said to be haunted by the ghost of a limping butler from an earlier era. He first appeared in 1937, well dressed and sporting the kind of luxurious whiskers that were by then decidedly outdated. A spectral waiter has also occasionally been spotted there but, like the butler, he reportedly dissolves into nothingness should anyone attempt to engage him in conversation.

3

Building London

'I don't know what London's coming to –
the higher the buildings, the lower the morals.'

Noël Coward

An Englishman's Home Is His . . .

. . . Castle

In Morden on Phipps Bridge Road, a small, one-bedroom flint tower, complete with crenellations and arrow slits, provides a surprising neighbour for an otherwise perfectly ordinary terrace.

. . . Former Public Loo

Architect Laura Clark recently converted some old council conveniences in Crystal Palace into a stylish subterranean apartment. With the average price of a London house forecast to reach £500,000 in the next few years, the 'bijou' abode includes a tiny private garden and an entire wall for displaying the owner's shoe collection. (In Fitzrovia, another former underground loo has been converted into a café bar called The Attendant.)

. . . Cossack Peasant's Hut

Thought to have been brought over from Russia for an international expo in the late nineteenth century, this traditional wooden '*izba*' now forms part of a family home in The Vale, Chelsea.

. . . Wren Church

London's tallest house, the tower of Christ Church Greyfriars has a view of St Paul's and includes three bedrooms and three bathrooms spread over a positively knee-knackering *eleven* floors. Fortunately, a small lift is provided, and three dead queens are buried in the garden.[1]

. . . Mini Skyscraper

With one room per floor, Joe Hagan's super-slim, seven-storey, steel-and-glass home looks like a scale model for a construction by Mies van der Rohe. It occupies a plot no larger than a lock-up garage on Golden Lane, just north of the Barbican.

. . . Shipping Container

Converted into brightly coloured, live-work spaces for artists, Container City at Trinity Buoy Wharf provides some of the most distinctive accommodation in London's reborn docklands.

---

1 In fact, the Square Mile boasts two more Wren churches that are being reused in this way. The tower of St Alban Tower, Wood Street, was converted into a bijou pied-à-terre in 1985 and, at the time of writing, the conversion of the Grade 1-listed St Mary Somerset is under way. The queens, incidentally, are Isabella of France, Marguerite of France and Joan of Scotland.

... Pub Yard

One of London's most compact family houses was created by architect Hugh Strange on just 75 square yards of disused land.

... Museum

Architect Sir John Soane left his house and its entire contents to the nation on the understanding that nothing would be added to his astonishing collection and absolutely nothing from it sold to pay the bills.

... Time Capsule

Within the shell of an old Spitalfields townhouse, the late Denis Severs, an American, re-created perfectly the atmosphere and feel of the seventeenth century and lived there 'with a candle, a chamber pot and a bedroll'.

... Tudor Palace

One of the contenders for central London's largest, non-royal private house, Crosby Hall dates back to the 1460s and originally stood in the Square Mile. In 1908, it was brought brick by brick to Chelsea, and has now been painstakingly restored by an insurance broker with a perfectionist's passion for all things Tudor.

Not the British Museum

London has some of the best museums in the world but also some of the strangest, from fans to bones to magic tricks and monsters:

The Fan Museum, Crooms Hill, Greenwich, SE10

The only museum in the world dedicated solely to fans. It's very good, but you can see why there aren't more of them.

The Museum of Brands, Colville Mews, W11

The perfect encapsulation of our modern consumerist culture, and a fascinating romp through packaging, advertising and how the hidden persuaders do their persuading.

London Fire Brigade Museum, Southwark Bridge Road, SE1

A new use for an old fire station, and every small boy's dream.

Magic Circle Museum, Stephenson Way, NW1

It's magic, literally.

Cuming Museum, Old Walworth Town Hall, Walworth Road, SE17

Napoleon's ceiling, pieces of the waistcoat Charles I was wearing when he was beheaded, and everything else of his father's that an eccentric Victorian son couldn't bear to see thrown away – or rather that portion of it that survived the devastating fire of 25 March 2013.

Hunterian Museum, Royal College of Surgeons, Lincoln's Inn Fields, WC2

Medical curiosities, scores of gruesome odds and sods from the path lab – and London's tallest human skeleton.

Horniman Museum, London Road, SE23

Stuffed animals, anthropology, musical instruments and a torture chair from the Spanish Inquisition.

The Anaesthesia Museum, Portland Place, W1

Three hundred years of 'It's a Knock-out'.

Grant Museum of Zoology, University Street, WC1

Jam-packed with more than 65,000 specimens – many of them in jam jars, and more than a few of them now extinct.

The Cinema Museum, Dugard Way, SE11

Literally a million historic film stills from the Ronald Grant Archive, together with London's largest collection of old usherette uniforms, posters, antique projectors and lots of authentic 1960s swirly carpet.

The Kirkaldy Testing Museum, Southwark Street, SE1

The home of David Kirkaldy's Victorian testing machine, designed to evaluate materials for strength and durability at a time when Britain was the workshop of the world.

Royal London Hospital Museum, Whitechapel Road, E1

Located in the crypt of a late nineteenth-century church, it commemorates Joseph Merrick, the Elephant Man, nurse Edith Cavell, and forensic medicine from the time of Jack the Ripper.

The London Sewing Machine Museum, Balham High Road, SW17

With more than 600 examples, including Charlie Chaplin's and another belonging to Princess Victoria, this is almost certainly south London's largest collection of sewing machines.

London's Earliest Skyscrapers

1314 – St Paul's Cathedral, EC4

Before the Great Fire, the City landmark dominated the landscape in a way Wren's magisterial replacement sadly hasn't done for years. Begun after an earlier conflagration (in 1087), at 585 ft it was the third-longest church in Europe and the spire reached an incredible 489 ft into the air. (By comparison, Wren's dome is just 278 ft high, and the building nearly 70 ft shorter overall.)

1420 – Southwark Cathedral, SE1

When the Old St Paul's was destroyed in September 1666, the title of London's tallest building passed to Southwark Cathedral, which at 163 ft retained the crown until 1710 when it was finally overtaken by Wren's builders.

1757 – Pagoda, Royal Botanic Gardens, Kew

The writer and aesthete Sir Horace Walpole hated it on sight and watching it go up complained that 'in a fortnight, you will be able to see it in Yorkshire'. He exaggerated slightly; at 163 ft it was an astonishing thing for the time but it has since been calculated that it would have needed to be nearly 80 times taller to be seen by Yorkshire folk from their back gardens.

1888 – Queen Anne's Mansions, SW1

Fourteen storeys and 116 ft high, banker Henry Hanley's block of luxury flats led to a change in the law when Queen Victoria expressed displeasure at it ruining her view of the Houses of Parliament. In 1894, a new London Building Act set an absolute limit of 80 ft, but unfortunately when Hanley's horror was pulled down in 1973, it was replaced by Basil Spence's much taller and even uglier Ministry of Justice.

1929 – 55 Broadway, SW1

At 174 ft, Charles Holden's London Transport HQ (now Transport for London) horrified firemen who said their ladders would not reach that high. As a result, the upper floors remained empty for years, and even now are used simply for archive storage.

1937 – Senate House, WC1

Another Charles Holden design, and the building English fascist leader Oswald Mosley planned to use as his parliament once he had taken over. The 210-ft monolith famously provided the model for Orwell's 'Ministry of Truth' in *Nineteen Eighty-Four* after the author had been employed there during the Second World War. (That such a prominent landmark survived the Blitz has encouraged speculation that it was a favourite of the Nazis and that, planning to use it when he had won the war, Hitler ordered the Luftwaffe to leave it alone.)

1952 – Shell-Mex House, WC2

Overlooking the Thames and with more than half a million square feet of floor space, Shell-Mex House was one of the largest buildings of its era. This 190-ft-high Art Deco masterpiece also boasts the two largest clock faces in the capital. Each clock has a diameter of 25 ft, and requires an electric motor the size of a family car to move the hands. However, neither chimes for fear of upstaging Big Ben.

LONDON'S SMALLEST LISTED BUILDING . . .

. . . is a small, brick-built hut for the Lincoln's Inn ostler. Dating back to 1860, when he would have been responsible for taking care of lawyers' and visitors' horses, the job was soon redundant as horsepower gradually supplanted the horse.

Estates of the Nation

On its completion in 1937, **Dolphin Square**, SW1, was the largest self-contained block of flats in Europe. With more than 1,250 apartments as well as a swimming pool, shopping arcade and restaurant, it has long been popular with politicians and, at its peak, was home to at least eighty Members of Parliament and the House of Lords. Princess Anne lived there briefly, too, making it one of London's more unusual royal residences.

Once home to comedians Tommy Trinder and Arthur Smith, **Du Cane Court** in Balham was completed in 1937 and is still the largest privately owned residential block in Europe. With 676 apartments, it is so large that, in 1940, pilots of the German air force were reportedly using it as a navigational aid on their bombing runs over London. (This revelation also prompted suggestions after the war that it had been designed by a Nazi sympathiser to look like a swastika from their air, but it wasn't and doesn't.)

Developed after the Great War by London County Council to provide much-needed 'Homes for Heroes', East London's **Becontree Housing Estate** is still thought to be the world's largest public housing project. With a starting population of more than 100,000 – including 25,000 children of school age – its construction was on such a scale that it required the laying of a new railway line and even a special wharf on the Thames.

Once considered the jewel in the crown of post-war public housing, the **Alton Estate** in Wandsworth was an attempt to re-create Le Corbusier's visionary but ill-conceived *Unité d'Habitation* in London. Instead, it was quickly recognised by film-makers as the perfect backdrop for dystopian dramas such as *Fahrenheit 451* and some of the seedier scenes in TV's *Minder* and *The Sweeney.* (Another utopian vision, Thamesmead, was similarly used as the seedy backdrop to *A Clockwork Orange.*)

Architectural modernist Erno Goldfinger famously moved his family to north Kensington and into his brutalist, concrete **Trellick Tower** – but only briefly before they returned to a lovely house overlooking leafy Hampstead Heath. Today, however, despite suffering many of the construction problems common to 1950s' and 1960s' system-built blocks, apartments here are highly sought-after and can command prices of around half a million pounds.

London's Maddest Buildings Never Built

1638 – The New Royal Palace

Inigo Jones's scheme to replace the old Palace of Whitehall was so vast that, had Charles I not been executed thereby rendering it redundant, it would have occupied a vast square stretching from Trafalgar Square down to the Ministry of Defence in one direction and in the other from the riverbank to halfway along the Mall.

1666 – The Other Monument

Much of the success of Wren's monument to the Great Fire depends on the elegance and simplicity of its fluted Doric column. Wren favoured something far more elaborate, however, and initially planned to top it with a 30-ft sculpture of a phoenix. Somewhat clumsily this was to signify the city's rebirth, but it was unwieldy and expensive – and potentially highly dangerous as the outstretched wings would have caught the wind.

1800 – London Double Bridge

George Dance proposed a pair of bridges instead of one, placed 100 yards apart, with drawbridge centre sections in order to allow large vessels through and decorative Egyptian detailing to celebrate the defeat of Napoleon in the Battle of the Nile two years earlier.

1815 – Trafalgar Square Pyramid

Intended to be the tallest structure in nineteenth-century London, this twenty-two-storey, 364-ft behemoth was designed by Philip and Matthew Cotes Wyatt. It would have covered the whole of Trafalgar Square but served no real purpose beyond commemorating the dead from the Napoleonic campaigns, and reinforcing our superiority over the French.

1824 – Grand National Cemetery

Covering more than 150 acres, at least forty of which were contained within an astonishing series of cloisters, Francis Goodwin's plan to redevelop either Shooters Hill or Primrose Hill as a 'city for the dead' included a replica of the Parthenon at its centre and no fewer than four copies of the Athenian Tower of the Winds.

1825 – Hyde Park Palace

Seeking to curry favour with an extravagant George IV, Frederick W. Trench MP proposed building a new royal home in Hyde Park with a two-mile ceremonial drive linking it to St Paul's Cathedral. A full 200 ft wide, and ramrod straight, the latter would have required the destruction of much of Mayfair, all of Covent Garden and most of the ancient buildings of Middle and Inner Temple. Colonel Trench admitted it was a 'splendid impossibility' but still recommended the idea to the Duke of Wellington.

1832 – Roman Colosseum

Modelled on the original, and by no means any smaller, John Goldicutt's massive rotunda was another design intended to occupy the whole of Trafalgar Square, this time to provide a permanent home for many of the learned societies now billeted at Somerset House and Burlington House on Piccadilly.

1861 – Crystal Palacc Monolith

Following the Prince Consort's death, and with no clear plans for the future of Crystal Palace, it was suggested the whole thing be retrieved from Sydenham and restored to Hyde Park by upending it to create a 1,000 ft-high glass obelisk.

1872 – High-Level Tower Bridge

Using hydraulics to winch the entire roadway more than 80 ft up into the air, Sidengham Duer's design was so far ahead of its time that, had it been built, it is highly doubtful many Victorians would have trusted the technology sufficiently to climb aboard.

1875 – Embankment Opera House

A naked attempt to out-Scala La Scala, this was to include its own Underground station and a tunnel linking it to the Palace of Westminster so that MPs could listen to 'beautiful music instead of dull debates'. Unfortunately, the foundations flooded badly, costing a fortune to rectify, and when that left insufficient funds to complete the project the £103,000 building was demolished at a cost of £3,000 and New Scotland Yard built on the site.

1889 – Non-Leaning Tower of Pisa

Constructed of solid granite, weighing an estimated 200,000 tons and costing more than £1,000,000, this replica of the Italian icon was designed to stand on a hilltop in Wembley. That it was never built is just one of the reasons why the name of architect Albert Brunel has never quite rivalled that of Isambard Kingdom Brunel or his son Marc.

1910 – King Edward VII Square

Requiring the wholesale destruction of Piccadilly Circus, John Murray's plans to commemorate the dead king would have replaced the world-famous figure of Eros[2] with a giant mounted statue of the late monarch and a heavily Edwardian 'National Opera House' in place of the area's cheerfully vulgar neon displays.

1918 – Selfridge's Mausoleum

Shortly after opening his magnificent new emporium on Oxford Street, Harry Gordon Selfridge commissioned Philip Tilden

2 In fact, it's not actually Eros (see Chapter 6 for details).

to design a monolithic tower to go on the top complete with a Greek-style temple at the summit and an honour guard of stone lions. Tilden came up with the goods, a structure that would have been more than 200 ft high, but warned the store owner that the weight of it would almost certainly cause the building beneath it to collapse.

1931 – King's Cross Airport

By placing a six-spoked, mile-wide 'wheel' above the station, Charles Glover's dream was to provide London with three intersecting runways. The idea was for plutocrats and the leisured rich to ascend into a bright technological future while the rest of London battled it out in the traffic down below.

1943 – Tower Bridge in Glass

The slightly mad brainchild of painter W. F. C. Holden, who thought the old bridge dowdy and old-fashioned and wished to see this much-loved London landmark re-created in streamlined glass and steel. He argued that it would save painting and repainting the old one, but fortunately with a war on no one took him seriously.

1967 – Regent Street Monorail

Determined to wreck what little elegance remains in the curving sweep of Regent Street, in the late 1960s the Greater London Council seriously considered building heavy concrete stanchions down the centre of the street in order to run two overhead monorails from Piccadilly up to Oxford Circus.

FIFTEEN FANTASTIC FOLLIES

Stoke Newington Pumping Station, N4

Based – pretty loosely, it has to be said – on Stirling Castle, the pumping station brought clean water into north London from Great Amwell in Hertfordshire. These days, it is an indoor mountaineering centre, which in its own way is just as bizarre as a Scottish castle in a London suburb.

Caledonian Clock Tower, N7

The last surviving portion of the once vast Caledonian Metropolitan Cattle Market is an Italianate, white-stone edifice. It towers over neighbouring playing fields and council estates, and dates back to 1855.

Holly Village, Highgate, N6

Baroness Burdett-Coutts was a notable nineteenth-century philanthropist, who built homes for the poor of east London and a vast covered market (now gone) because she felt sorry for the cold, wet costermongers. In Highgate, she built a small cluster of Gothic cottages around a green, but these were for the better off and today command the kind of high prices that individualistic houses in cities warrant.

Crocker's Folly, Aberdeen Place, NW8

Convinced a new railway terminal would be built at St John's Wood, a nineteenth-century speculator of this name built a large railway hotel only to see the trains continue all the way into London. He lost his shirt, and his Crown Hotel – now semi-derelict – has been known by its cruel nickname ever since.

Trobidge Castle, Buck Lane, NW9

In the 1920s, architect Ernest Trobridge pioneered an efficient means of building modern prefabricated houses, but his personal preference was for something more traditional. Acquiring land in Kingsbury, he built a series of mock-medieval flats and some fake Tudor cottages, none of them at all convincing but quaint rather than queer and quite sought-after.

Queen's Tower, SW7

At nearly 300 ft, London's tallest folly is also its least known, being largely invisible to anyone walking by. It was designed by T. E. Colcutt (architect of the Savoy Hotel) as part of the Imperial Institute in the heyday of 'Albertopolis'. Today, it is the only part still standing, marooned in the middle of Imperial College and best seen from Kensington Gardens.

St Antholin's Spire, Round Hill, SE26

With its unusual octagonal spire, St Antholin's was regarded as one of Wren's finest city churches but was nevertheless pulled down in 1875 to make way for Queen Victoria Street. The spire was rescued and found its way to a country estate in Kent, only to be swallowed up as London expanded southwards and a suburb grew up around it.

Obelisk, Tibbet's Corner, SW15

Commemorates the erection in the 1770s of London's first fire-proof house, which had metal plates inserted between the floorboards to retard the spread of any flames. The house sadly disappeared long ago and – as is only to be expected – is said locally to have burned to the ground.

Farm House, Farm Street, W1

Once home to actress Gloria Swanson and Thelma Lady Furness, who introduced Wallis Simpson to the Prince of Wales. This mock-Tudor house is only 100 years old but was built using genuinely old stone flags and authentically medieval doors and panelling, and so looks the part.

22–24 Leinster Gardens, W2

No more real than a film set, the façades of two typical Bayswater terraced houses were built to conceal a railway line running behind them. Today, this forms part of the District Line, but before electrification the large opening behind the houses allowed for smoke from steam locomotives to escape the shallow tunnels.

Burton's Tent, North Worple Way, Mortlake

In an otherwise ordinary cemetery, the tomb of the explorer Sir Richard Burton takes the form of an Arab tent decorated with a combination of Christian and Moorish symbols and with a small window at the rear for the curious to peer in. His wife would have preferred Westminster Abbey, but with Sir Richard having abandoned Christianity (and embraced pornography with considerable enthusiasm) the church authorities were not to be persuaded.

The Rotunda, Green Hill, SE18

For many years a splendid home for 'the military curiosities usually preserved in the Repository of the Royal Regiment of Artillery' – that is to say, hundreds of old guns – this charming building was designed by John Nash to celebrate the defeat of Napoleon. It takes the form of a mock tent, which originally stood in St James's Park.

Royal Naval College Gates, SE10

Built to mark Admiral Lord Anson's successful near-four-year circumnavigation in the 1740s, the piers are surmounted by a pair of globes showing the terrestrial and celestial spheres. Now, sadly, too corroded to read, they are 6 ft in diameter and cost more than 40 guineas apiece at a time when a cabin boy would have had to have worked for twenty years to earn a similar sum.

The Bathhouse, Bishopsgate Churchyard, EC4

In recent years housing a café, an Indian restaurant and an Italian pizzeria, one of the City's most curious little buildings was originally an elaborately tiled Turkish *hamam* until the Victorian fad for steam baths gradually faded.

Severndroog Castle, Shooter's Hill, SE18

Hidden among the trees in Oxleas Wood is a triangular Gothic tower built to commemorate the life of Commodore Sir William James, Bt. (1721–83). An officer of the East India Company, its evocative name is an Anglicised reference to his conquest of the Indian fortress of Savarnadurg (off the coast of Goa) and the successful routing of the pirates operating in its vicinity.

4
Spy's London

'The Secret Intelligence Service I knew occupied dusky suites of little rooms opposite St James's Park Tube Station.'

John le Carré

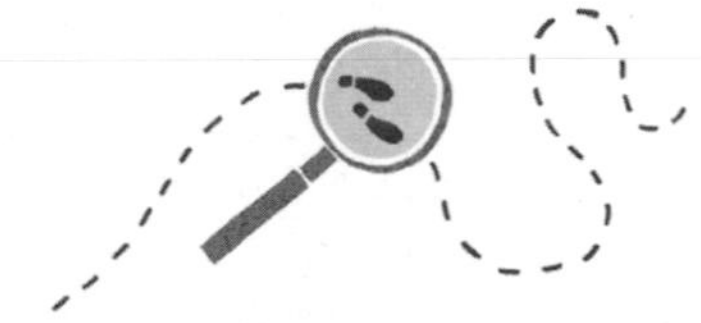

Famous Buildings with Secret Histories

Sir Winston Churchill's wartime hotline to the White House required so much equipment to encrypt and transmit messages across the Atlantic that there was insufficient space for it all at the **Cabinet War Rooms** beneath Whitehall. Instead, some 55 tons of special, top-secret technology was housed beneath Oxford Street in the basement of Selfridges, the store even taking on a detachment of armed marines to take care of security.

Throughout the Cold War, the grounds of **Holy Trinity Church** in Knightsbridge provided the location for so-called 'dead letter drops', a safe place where the KGB could leave secret messages for Soviet agents based in the capital. (Brompton Oratory nearby fulfilled a similar function.)

In the 1940s, **Electra House**, a huge Edwardian edifice that occupies much of one side of Moorgate in the City, housed the mysterious 'Dept EH'. This was a division of the wartime Special Operations Executive (SOE) and was charged with bugging foreign embassies and producing and disseminating propaganda designed to undermine enemy operations in Europe.

Claridge's in Brook Street, Mayfair – long popular with foreign royalty and Heads of State – was reportedly used to test a device developed by the Post Office for MI5. This enabled a telephone to be used to eavesdrop on conversations in the rooms of particular guests at the hotel, but unfortunately the scheme was leaked to the Russians before it could be put into operation.

Overlooking the Mall, **2 Carlton Gardens** was the location for a meeting in 1954 where MI6 and the CIA agreed to cooperate on the construction of a tunnel beneath the Berlin Wall. The idea was to intercept hundreds of thousands of telephone calls made to, from or within the Soviet sector, but unfortunately the existence of the 1,500-ft-long tunnel was immediately blown by George Blake (see page 49) who was present at the meeting.

REAL PLACES WITH FICTIONAL SPY CONNECTIONS

At the foot of Westminster Bridge, set into the plinth of the South Bank Lion, a doorway (which exists) leads to Vauxhall Cross Station (which doesn't) in the 007 thriller, *Die Another Day.*

Freemasons' Hall in Great Queen Street, WC2, was used as the MI5 headquarters in the television series *Spooks*.

Boodle's in St James's Street, SW1, is the model for Blade's, the gentleman's club where James Bond lunches frugally with his boss, Sir Miles Messervy ('M').

In *Billion Dollar Brain*, the opening sequence was shot near King's Cross Station, with 297 Pentonville Road standing in for Harry Palmer's office.

In *Die Another Day*, Bond squares up to Gustav Graves in an (imaginary) fencing salon at the Reform Club in Pall Mall, SW1.

Blythe House, Blythe Road, W14, provided the setting for the Circus, the MI6 headquarters in the film adaptation of John le Carré's novel *Tinker Tailor Soldier Spy*. Originally the London headquarters of the Post Office Savings Bank, the late Victorian building is now used for storing surplus exhibits from the Science Museum, British Museum and the V&A.

TEN TWENTIETH-CENTURY TRAITORS

1933 – Norman Baillie-Stewart

Court-martialled at Chelsea Barracks under the Official Secrets Act, in 1933 Baillie-Stewart was found guilty of selling military secrets to a foreign power. Having reportedly fallen in love with a German woman, and deciding to take German citizenship, he had been persuaded to spy for them instead and had stolen some experimental tank blueprints from army files at Aldershot.

In wartime, he would undoubtedly have been sentenced to the death penalty for this, but instead he faced a theoretical maximum of 140 years in jail on a total of ten charges. In the end, he spent just five years locked in the Tower of London – the last Briton to serve a sentence there – before fleeing to mainland Europe before the war started. He died in Dublin in 1966, having changed his name to James Scott.

1940 – Archibald Maule Ramsay

The only Member of Parliament to be interned during the Second World War, Ramsay was commissioned into the Coldstream Guards after Eton and Sandhurst. Elected to Westminster in 1931, he was generally well liked but never entirely trusted and rose no higher than a government position on the Potato Marketing Board.

In the late 1930s he began to voice increasingly pro-Nazi views and, like many others who shared his views at the time, became convinced that the Conservative Party was being controlled by a Jewish cabal. His response was to establish the rival Right Club and, later, to attempt to reinstate a thirteenth-century law introduced by Edward I banning all Jews from England. In 1940, after becoming involved with a suspected spy at the US Embassy, he was incarcerated in Brixton Prison.

1945 – John Amery

The Old Harrovian son and brother of British MPs, Amery amassed an impressive seventy-four motoring convictions before joining the Fascists in the Spanish Civil War. In 1941, he was recruited by the Nazis and began making pro-German broadcasts from Berlin in the hope of encouraging British internees to change sides.

Towards the end of the war, he joined Mussolini and, following his capture by Italian partisans, was handed over to the British. Interviewed by MI5 and charged with treason, Amery pleaded guilty in a trial that lasted just eight minutes. Sent to Wandsworth Prison, he was hanged after telling the hangman, Albert Pierrepoint, how much he had been looking forward to their meeting.

1946 – Lord Haw-Haw

Britain's most famous traitor always argued he was no such thing, as William Joyce was born in Brooklyn, NY, to parents who had taken US citizenship. He was educated in England, however, and lied about his age to join the Royal Worcester Regiment before falling under the spell of Oswald Mosley's British Union of Fascists.

In 1940, he took German citizenship and spent much of the war broadcasting anti-British propaganda under the call-sign 'Germany Calling'. Captured by British forces in northern Germany at the war's end, Joyce was brought back to London, tried and, on 3 January 1946, hanged at Wandsworth.

1946 – Theodore Schurch

A day after Lord Haw-Haw's execution, Hammersmith-born Schurch was hanged at Pentonville, the only British soldier to be executed for treachery throughout the whole of the Second World War. After defecting in order to spy for the enemy, his crimes included posing as a PoW to gain the trust of other prisoners before betraying them to the Germans. Today, Schurch also enjoys the distinction of being the last person to be executed in Britain for a crime other than murder.

1951 – Burgess and Maclean

Espionage's most famous double act, Old Etonian Guy Burgess and Donald Maclean, met at Cambridge. Quickly recruited to the Russian cause, the pair began moving effortlessly toward the higher echelons of the Foreign Office, Diplomatic Corps, MI5 and the BBC. Soon, Maclean had access to atomic secrets, and Burgess was well placed as a Second Secretary at the embassy in Washington.

In 1951, Burgess was recalled to London for 'serious misconduct' and, tipped off by Philby (see page 50), the two immediately fled the country. Burgess died in Moscow, a drunk aged fifty-two, and Maclean followed him twenty years later. Bizarrely, the latter's ashes were brought back to the country he had betrayed, and scattered at Penn in Buckinghamshire.

1961 – George Blake

A British spy who became a double-agent for the USSR, Blake's duplicity only came to light when he was exposed by a Polish defector. Sentenced to forty-two years in prison – still a record for any British court, but then he was conceivably our deadliest traitor – Blake was sprung from Wormwood Scrubs in west London by a fellow inmate, assisted by two anti-nuclear campaigners.

Via a safe house at 28 Highlever Road, London W10, Blake was spirited away to Moscow concealed in a hidden compartment of a campervan. A committed Marxist-Leninist, at the time of writing he was still living in that city and drawing a regular KGB pension. He is thought to have given away the identities of up to 400 agents, but continues to deny that he was ever a traitor and, as recently as 2007 (when he was awarded the Russian Order of Friendship), insisted that 'to betray, you first have to belong. I never belonged.'

1963 – Kim Philby

Born in the Raj to British parents, Philby became a communist while a student at Cambridge in the 1930s. Recruited as a Soviet agent at that time, he secured a position with the British Secret Intelligence Service, ironically as the head of anti-communist counter-espionage.

Posted to Washington after the war, as First Secretary at the British Embassy he was responsible for liaison with the CIA from 1949 to 1951. He later moved to the Middle East and, in 1963, after protesting his innocence to the press on a visit to his mother's flat in Grove Court, South Kensington, he disappeared. Resurfacing in Moscow, he was granted Soviet citizenship and remained there until his death in 1988.

1964 – Anthony Blunt

Surveyor of the Queen's Pictures before he was identified as a Soviet double-agent, Blunt made a private confession in 1964. Even so, it was to be fifteen years before he was publicly exposed as the 'fourth man' (in Andrew Boyle's book, *Climate of Treason*) and named as such by PM Margaret Thatcher.

The public outrage was palpable – not least at the justifiable sense that there had been an Establishment cover-up – and the Queen moved quickly to strip him of his knighthood. His boyfriend subsequently fell from a sixth-floor balcony after a row and, never recovering from the disgrace of his exposure, the reviled Blunt finally died of heart failure in 1983 at his home at Portsea Place, W2.

London's Killing Fields

The Millennium Hotel, Grosvenor Square, SW1

In 2006, a former member of the Russian Federal Security Service, Alexander Litvinenko, had a cup of tea at the hotel. He later died of radioactive poisoning, and it is now thought that during Litvinenko's visit to the hotel an unidentified foreign agent was able to secrete a tiny particle of polonium-210 into his teapot.

Waterloo Bridge, SE1

On his way to work at the BBC, the Bulgarian dissident Georgi Markov was fatally poisoned using a specially adapted umbrella that deposited a tiny pellet of highly toxic ricin into his leg.

24 Carlton House Terrace, SW1

In 2007, having been outed as a longstanding agent for the Israeli secret service Mossad, the Egyptian businessman Ashraf Marwan fell to his death from his balcony. Still treated as suspicious, his death has never been explained.

Shellbourne Hotel, 1 Lexham Gardens, W8

In 1952, Polish-born Christine Granville was stabbed to death at the hotel. Despite her wartime heroics as a highly effective and much decorated SOE agent, it was a crime of passion rather than a professional hit. A friend of Ian Fleming's, Granville is thought to have provided the model for at least two Bond girls, Vespa Lynd and Tatiana Romanova. Her murderer, Dennis Muldowney, was hanged at Pentonville on 30 September 1952.

Tower of London

Charged with 'committing treachery in that you at Ramsay in Huntingdonshire on the night of 31 January 1941 / 1 February 1941 descended by parachute with intent to help the enemy . . .' Joseph Jakobs was the last person ever to be executed at the Tower. He was dispatched by an eight-man firing squad at precisely 7.12am on 15 August 1941.

31 Pembroke Gardens, W8

A drunken spendthrift with a shocking drugs habit, cipher clerk Ernest Oldham paid for his extravagant lifestyle by spying for Stalin's secret police, the OGPU. In 1932, he lost his job at the Foreign Office due to his unreliability, and no longer of any use was bumped off the following year. His death was disguised as a suicide, and it suited both sides to reach a verdict that he had, in fact, killed himself by sticking his head in the oven.

The Bandstand, Clapham Common, SW4

Found beaten to death in 1911, burglar and petty thief Leon Beron's body was distinguished by the letter 'S', which was deeply carved into each cheek. Though no one was ever charged or found guilty for the crime, it has long been supposed he was killed by anarchists after being uncovered as a police spy.

END OF AN ERA

Long after the death penalty was abolished in this country for relatively ordinary offences such as murder, it remained on the statute books for the very special crime of high treason. At Wandsworth Prison, the country's last set of gallows was kept oiled and ready until as recently as 1994, and it was not until 1998 that the law was finally changed. Spies and other traitors now face being simply locked up with the rest of the criminal fraternity.

5

Under London

'London always reminds me of a brain. It is similarly convoluted and circuitous . . . a labyrinth, full of turnings and twistings, just like a brain.'

James Geary

From pipes to plague pits, through tombs and tunnels to private railways, vast underground office complexes and bunkers large enough to shelter 12,000 people at a time, the London that lies hidden beneath the one we know seems not much smaller and many times more mysterious.

Government Moles

Much is made these days about the need for government transparency, but whenever our democratically elected rulers feel the need to slip beneath the radar, you can be sure they have plenty of places where they can disappear:

Storey's Gate

Protected by a 17-ft concrete shield – this can be seen at ground level from St James's Park – an estimated 6 acres of space, more than 200 offices in total, were excavated beneath the Treasury in the run-up to the Second World War. Like an iceberg, only a tiny part is visible to the public – namely Churchill's Cabinet War Rooms – but the authorities prefer to remain tight-lipped about the remainder, which lies hidden below. (During his wartime service, the comedian Norman Wisdom was stationed down there, but he was removed and put on a charge after addressing the PM as 'Winnie' and subsequently never gave away any secrets.)

Post Office Tunnels

Even now, the true extent of these is unclear, although the original plan was to link the aforementioned Whitehall complex to other top-secret facilities near St Paul's, at Covent Garden, Waterloo and Moorgate. Codenamed Citadel, Bastion, Rampart and Fortress, these outposts were no sooner completed than rendered redundant when the Russians developed their own nuclear armoury.

Three Citadels

In the early 1930s, convinced that another war with Germany was inevitable, three secret command centres were excavated deep beneath north London. These were at Cricklewood, Harrow and Dollis Hill – the last named being buried deep beneath the innocuous-sounding Post Office Research Station. This was a facility charged with devising new techniques for bugging foreign embassies and consulates in the capital, but has recently been converted into flats.

Beneath the Squares

Between the wars, beneath Lincoln's Inn Fields, and Queen, Russell, Bloomsbury and Woburn squares, the London County Council excavated many thousands of yards of deep trenches. These were protected by concrete and earth banking, and air-locked against gas attack, but little is known about what became of them following Germany's defeat.

LONDON'S MOST INTRIGUING CRYPTS

All Hallows-by-the-Tower, EC3

Also known as All Hallows Barking and occasionally St Mary's, the building is built on the foundations of a Saxon church and was rumoured to be the final resting place of the heart of Richard the Lionheart. More certain is the existence of a small museum of Roman and Saxon artefacts in the crypt, including an outstandingly well-preserved section of Roman tessellated pavement.

St John's Waterloo, SE1

With marshy ground requiring much deeper-than-usual foundations, this nineteenth-century church has a vast crypt, although the latter is only rarely opened to the public. Originally intended for prestigious interments, it was more or less gutted after the church was bombed in the 1940s. Bizarrely, an open pipe in the floor shows how close to the surface the water table lies, an ongoing concern as this vast stone edifice is supported by 200-year-old oak piles.

Carmelite Monastery, Magpie Alley, EC4

Encapsulated beneath a modern office building, but visible behind a large picture window, is a surviving fragment of what was once a mighty religious foundation. From 1253, the Carmelite Order of the White Friars held a large plot of land between Fleet Street and the Thames, on which were built a church, cloisters, cemetery and herb and vegetable gardens. Following the depredations of Henry VIII, this small portion was used as a coal cellar, but is now safely preserved for all to see.

St Pancras New Church, NW1

Crypt burials were always popular among the well-to-do and remained so until they were outlawed in London in 1854. By then, 557 bodies had been interred beneath this busy church and, today, the space – which during two world wars served as an air-raid shelter – has been remodelled as an unusual but popular art gallery.

St Bride's, Fleet Street, EC4

This was such a popular place for burials that, when his brother died, Pepys had to bribe the sexton to 'justle together' the bodies to make room. Archaeological enquiries here have uncovered evidence of at least seven different churches dating back nearly 1,400 years, and what is almost certainly London's first community of Irish settlers. Occasional guided tours take in the charnel house and ossuary, an unusually grim discovery to find beneath the modern city.

Ministry of Defence, Whitehall, SW1

A unique secular crypt, and the last surviving remnant of Cardinal Wolsey's magnificent riverside palace at York

Place. Following its acquisition by Henry VIII, this was incorporated into Whitehall Palace, the spacious undercroft becoming the king's private wine cellar. Somehow it survived the massive fire that destroyed the Palace in 1698, but was then more or less forgotten until work started on the new ministry building in the 1930s. Now safely encased in a protective collar of reinforced concrete, one of London's most fascinating Tudor relics is sadly not ordinarily open to view.

St John Clerkenwell, EC1

A precious survivor of the same king's ransacking and destruction of the monasteries, Clerkenwell's famous St John's Gate was built in 1504 by Sir Thomas Docwra and formed part of Clerkenwell Priory, the English wing of the Knights Hospitallers of St John of Jerusalem. Latterly, it became a tavern and then the headquarters for the St John Ambulance Association, but it was substantially rebuilt after being badly damaged by enemy action in the 1940s. Because of this, the Norman crypt of the nearby church of St John is now the oldest and most authentic part remaining of the old priory, a small but beautiful and exquisitely decorated Early English structure. The church itself, though much restored since, escaped destruction at the Dissolution as Henry VIII used it to store his hunting tents.

London's Lost Rivers

London's rapid expansion from medieval times onwards means that once pretty streams rapidly degraded into open sewers and were then converted into closed ones. Happily, their names are often commemorated in the streets and residential areas above, meaning their courses can be traced although the rivers themselves are rarely if ever seen.

Earl's Sluice

This rises near Denmark Hill and flows into the Thames at Rotherhithe after joining the River Peck (which gives its name to Peckham). The mouth is by Surrey Quays, where once old whalers used to tie up. The earl in question is Robert Fitzroy, an illegitimate son of Henry I.

The Effra

Flowed from Upper Norwood through Dulwich and Brockwell Park into Brixton and then beneath Oval Tube Station. It joins the Thames at Vauxhall, but does little to justify its name, which is a Celtic word meaning 'torrent'.

The Fleet

The most famous of the missing rivers rises on Hampstead Heath (close to the bathing ponds) and travels downhill via King's Cross, Holborn and Clerkenwell to join the Thames at Blackfriars. The name is from the Anglo-Saxon for estuary – '*fleot*'.

The Grand Surrey Canal

Intended to link the county with the capital, this freightway reached no further than Peckham before it was overtaken by the railways. It closed in 1971 and has since been largely filled in.

The Neckinger

From 'devil's neckinger' – hangman's slang for the noose – this rises close to the Imperial War Museum, passes by Elephant and Castle and through Bermondsey to enter the Thames near St Saviour's Dock.

The Tyburn

This rises in Haverstock Hill and flows through Marylebone, down what is now Avery Row in Mayfair, past Shepherd Market and beneath Buckingham Palace. A small section can be seen in the basement of Grays Antiques on Davies Street, and the outflow beneath Pimlico's Grosvenor Road is readily identified from the opposite bank of the Thames.

The Walbrook

Long an important source of fresh water for the City, the Walbrook entered the Square Mile close to All Hallows London Wall – hence the name – and joins the Thames west of Cannon Street Station. Now called the London Bridge Sewer, its fate has matched those of most of London's forgotten waterways.

The Westbourne

With its origins in Hampstead and the short-lived Kilburn Spa, the river flowed through Maida Vale and Bayswater and into Hyde Park. Partly dammed to create Long Water, it then flows beyond Sloane Square – travelling over the station platforms in a pipe – and enters the Thames by Chelsea Bridge.

Grosvenor Canal

Only a few hundred yards long, in the 1820s London's shortest canal served the Chelsea Waterworks Company, which incurred royal displeasure when its steam pump sent noxious fumes over Buckingham Palace. It was the first to use iron pipes in place of leaky wooden ones until new regulations outlawed using Thames water for domestic supplies. One end of the canal then disappeared beneath platforms 15–19 at Victoria Station, but part of an old arch through which barges once passed can still be seen by Bridge House on Ebury Bridge Road.

THE ENVY OF THE WORLD?

The famously irrepressible Mayor of London Boris Johnson[1] described the Tube with typical gusto on its 150th birthday as 'the throbbing cardiovascular system of the greatest city on earth'. Elsewhere, its importance to London has been likened to the metal thread running through a banknote – always there, taken for granted, but essential to its value. But the world's first and oldest underground railway has also attracted less favourable descriptions too, none of which will surprise regular commuters.

Passengers felt 'as if they had been chewing Lucifer matches' according to the *Yorkshire Herald*, providing readers with an impression of what it was like to travel on one of the very first Underground trains 150 years ago.

'A form of mild torture which no person would undergo if he could conveniently help it' wrote *The Times*, reporting on the completion of the Circle Line in 1884.

'Prisoners will be condemned to so many continuous round trips as they are now to so many weeks in jail.' This

1 For more from him, see Chapter 18.

was also a reference to the Circle Line, with the *Pall Mall Gazette* offering up a suggestion to help reduce prison overcrowding.

'An experience of Hades' said the editor of the *Daily Express,* whose son later went on to become chairman of London Transport.

'The Sardine Box Railway' reported the magazine *Punch*, commenting on the claustrophobically enclosed carriages on the City & South London Line. This opened in 1890, the world's first electric underground railway, and ran from Stockwell to the City.

'We have scarcely yet been educated up to that condition of social equality when lords and ladies will be content to ride side by side with Billingsgate fish fags and Smithfield butchers.' This view was published in the *Railway Times* following the decision not to offer separate accommodation for first-, second- and third-class passengers.

'Young girls and men are crowded in such a way that the question of decency even comes up.' W. J. Kelley MP questioned the morality of the railway during a debate in the House of Commons in the mid-1930s.

'Commuters face a daily trauma and are forced to travel in intolerable conditions' concluded a 2004 Parliamentary report, which surprised no one at all who has ever been on a rush-hour train.

'Why preserve these London Underground hell holes?' screamed the *Daily Telegraph* in 2011, on hearing that a total of 72 stations on the network were listed as Grade II or II*. According to the paper, every effort should go not into preserving the system as an historical artefact but in making it as efficient as possible in terms of moving millions from A to B.

Little wonder, then, that at the opening of the Metropolitan Railway in 1863, the Prime Minister declined even to attempt a journey on it. Instead, Lord Palmerston, who to be fair was approaching his eightieth birthday, let it be known that he wished to spend as much time as possible above ground.

Voices on the Underground

Inspector Sands

In fact, you never hear him speak, but any announcement referring to 'Inspector Sands' is a coded warning to station staff of an incident – possibly a fire or suspect package – somewhere in the station.

Sonia

The nickname given by male station staff to all female announcers on the network's public address system, because 'her voice gets sonia nerves'.

Tim Bentinck

David Archer from the famous BBC radio soap – more correctly the 12th Earl of Portland and 8th Count Bentinck und Waldeck-Limpurg – provides the voice behind the famous 'Mind the Gap' warnings at Piccadilly Line stations.

Oswald Laurence

Another actor provided the 'Mind the Gap' voice for the Northern Line. After more than forty years, Laurence's recordings were phased out, but then brought back in to use (at Embankment Station in 2013) after reports that his widow had expressed her disappointment at never hearing his voice again.

Other Underground Oddities

Holborn Tramway Station

London's trams stopped running in the 1950s but this station beneath Kingsway was left intact. It is one of the last surviving relics of the Kingsway Tram Subway, a cut-and-cover tunnel designed to provide a link between north and south London trams networks without adding to traffic congestion at street level. Occasionally open to the public, the entrance can still be seen behind locked gates in the centre of Southampton Row.

Camden Catacombs, London

Hidden beneath Camden Lock's famous market and what was once an old gin warehouse, this extensive web of vaults and subterranean passageways originally provided stabling, storage and tack space for scores of pit ponies serving the railway/canal interchange situated above. Mostly closed to the public, some sections can be seen while visiting the market.

As well as an underground canal basin large enough for narrow boats to turn round, the complex includes a vast hall that housed steam-powered winding gear to winch trains up the hill from Euston Station. As such, it provides a fascinating glimpse of changing transport technologies in the metropolis – from horses through canals to rail.

Nursemaid's Tunnel

One you won't find on any map, this small foot-tunnel runs

from Park Square Gardens, NW1, beneath the Euston Road to Crescent Gardens, W1. Both are privately owned parks, meaning that the tunnel linking Camden and Westminster is restricted to residents and other key-holders only, although the public is occasionally allowed a peek during the annual London Open Gardens Weekend.

Tower Subway, London

A rare, privately owned tunnel beneath the Thames, this was completed in 1868 but is still in use today. The entrance on the north bank is a small cylindrical building just west of the Tower of London, and originally cable cars were run from here to Southwark and back again. Unfortunately, these were so slow that passengers preferred to walk through the tunnel and were charged a ha'penny to do so.

When Tower Bridge opened in 1894, people could cross at no cost, and the operators rapidly lost their custom. The tunnel was subsequently sold to the London Hydraulic Power Company, and until the 1970s it formed part of an incredible 200-mile network of tunnels, pipes and ducts that channelled hydraulic power around London to raise theatre curtains, cranes, hotel lifts and so on. Today, more mundanely, it is used to run fibre-optic cables under the Thames and is closed to the public.

Admiralty Citadel, London

The big, ivy-covered building at the end of the Mall is essentially a massive wartime pillbox whose blast-proof walls have proved too strong and too costly to demolish. What Churchill called in his war memoirs 'that vast monstrosity which weighs upon Horse Guards Parade' conceals several layers of top-secret, subterranean offices that are still thought to be in use.

It is also rumoured to be linked by tunnel to Buckingham Palace, providing a useful refuge should things turn nasty and the Royal Family need to flee, but naturally this has not been confirmed. (For years, it was said the tunnel could be glimpsed through a vent in the Gents' loos at the Institute of Contemporary Arts, but again there is no proof of this.)

Thames Water Ring Main

Diving deeper underground than most of the Tube, almost twice as long as the Channel Tunnel, and easily wide enough to drive a train through, this pumps 300 million gallons a day of fresh water around London. It cost more than £250 million when it was completed in the mid-1990s and, in theory, could fill an Olympic swimming pool in under two minutes.

The Greenwich Foot Tunnel

Linking London's newest royal borough to the Isle of Dogs and the docks, this is reached via wood-panelled Edwardian lifts descending from two splendid, glass-domed entrance pavilions. At the northern end, it narrows sharply as a result of emergency repairs to wartime bomb damage, and while it officially forms part of the National Cycle Network, cyclists are forbidden to ride through the tunnel.

Mail Rail

From 1927 to 2003, the Post Office had its own railway network running through nearly seven miles of private tunnels with eight stations taking it from Paddington to Whitechapel. Some fifty driverless electric trains connected the major sorting offices and transported up to 30,000 items daily, with a train running every five minutes during peak times. After a brief appearance as the

Italian 'Poste Vaticane' in the Bruce Willis film *Hudson Hawk*, it was offered for sale following the closure – but with no takers so far.

The Eisenhower Centre

Situated on Chenies Street just off Tottenham Court Road, the exceptionally ugly, windowless silo is the above-ground portion of one of the London's eight Deep Level Shelters. These were excavated in the early 1940s beneath the stations at Chancery Lane, Clapham South, Clapham Common, Clapham North, Stockwell, Goodge Street, Camden Town and Belsize Park.

Each comprises twin tunnels more than 16 ft in diameter and an astonishing 1,200 ft long, with room for 8,000 people to shelter during an air raid. Four were set aside for civilian use, with four more designed as secret military command centres, including this one, which was reserved for the American Allied commander's personal use. All eight still exist and are occasionally offered for sale, but with a clause in the lease permitting the government to reoccupy the tunnels in the event of another war.

SEWERS – THE LOAD THAT DARE NOT SPEAK ITS NAME

Before sewers, cities had cesspits, tens of thousands of them, and the unpleasant task of emptying these could make rich men of so-called rakers and gong-farmers. In the fourteenth century, these chaps could charge up to £2 a job, at a time when a peasant would be doing well to earn just two pence a day.

The price reflected not just the unpleasantness of the task but also the danger, one raker at the time drowning 'monstrously in his own excrement', while two more succumbed to toxic fumes while trying to retrieve a barrel of booze that had somehow slipped down the flue.

Determined to improve things, Henry III built the first public loos since Roman times, but they were expensive – in 1383 the one at London Bridge cost £11 – and Londoners objected to footing the bill. They preferred to carry on as they were, and by 1388 a new law was brought in specifically outlawing any act likely to 'corrupt or pollute ditches, rivers and the air of London'.

It took until 1531 for Henry VIII to create official Commissioners of Sewers, but it was only when a way was found to make poo pay that anyone took a real interest in the stuff. The war with Spain from 1585 to 1604 boosted the demand for gunpowder, and when it was discovered that useful nitrates could be extracted from excrement, 'saltpetremen' were empowered by the government to enter any house and remove any waste they thought they could sell on.

Efficient sewers were still a good way off, though, and nearly everything unpleasant continued to be flushed into the Thames. By the start of the nineteenth century, a million Londoners were still relying on an estimated 200,000 cesspits, and it took several major outbreaks of cholera – just one of which killed more than 10,000 people – before it was finally decided to do something sensible about London's big problem.

Briefly there was talk of piping much of the effluent out to market gardeners in Hammersmith, and plans to dry the remainder so it could be sold to farmers. But in 1859 it was finally accepted there would be a cost to the clean-up rather than a profit, and the engineering genius Sir Joseph Bazalgette was brought in to create the massive sewer system on which London still relies.

Bazalgette's masterplan was based on a network of six vast 'interceptory' sewers, each one egg-shaped in cross section, so that water lower down would move faster and self-clean the pipes. As this suggests, Bazalgette seemed to have thought of everything, even employing special Staffordshire Blue bricks (formulated to withstand the effects of a constant flow of sewage) and a new Portland cement that actually hardened over time.

In all, he built more than 100 miles of these broad sewers, enough to drain 450 miles of main sewers and 13,000 miles of local ones. In so doing, his project consumed nearly 320 million bricks, 880,000 cubic yards of concrete, and required the excavation of 3.5 million cubic yards of earth – but it was as simple as it was elegant and, most of all, it worked.

Powered almost entirely by gravity, the network successfully removed millions of tons of waste out to treatment plants at Beckton and Plumstead, and finally solved a problem that was – quite literally – as old as London itself. Admittedly, it had cost more than £4 million and took nearly seventeen years to complete, but to do the same today would cost billions – and the chances are we'd get it wrong.

6

Monumental London

'If you're curious, London's an amazing place.'

David Bailey

Lifting the Lid on Nelson's Column

Strictly speaking it should be called 'The Nelson Column', and allowing for inflation it cost just over £4 million in today's terms. A quarter of the cost was met by the Russian Tsar, the largest single contributor.

The pre-eminent English hero died in 1805, but it took another thirty-two years even to form a committee to consider how to commemorate his life and outstanding achievements. Eventually, a competition was held, and it was won by William Railton who proposed building a massive Corinthian column weighing more than 2,500 tons. The result was controversial, however, so the competition had to be re-run with Railton being again declared the winner and awarded £200 for his idea.

The runner-up was Edward Hodges Bailey. As a consolation prize, he was asked to sculpt the figure of Lord Nelson, facing south towards the Channel.

The first stone wasn't laid until 1840, when the ceremonials were conducted by Charles Davison Scott, son of Nelson's secretary John Scott.

The column was still unfinished four years later, however, as the money had run out. Forced to take over the project, the government insisted that 30 ft be trimmed off the column to save money.

The 18 ft-1 in. figure of Nelson nevertheless weighed in at a hefty 18 tons, and was expertly carved from a huge piece of Craigleith sandstone donated by the Duke of Buccleuch. It was described by one envious Frenchman as 'hideous . . . like a rat impailed on a stick', but actually Bailey's carving is so detailed that the word 'NILE' can still be read on one of his medals. Curiously, he left off the eye-patch we all know and love, although the Admiral is at least shown with one arm missing.

The lions at the base were not completed until 1867, more than sixty years after Nelson's death, and Sir Edwin Landseer was awarded the commission only because the now relatively unknown John Graham Lough turned the job down.

Finally completed, in 1896 the figure at the top was struck by a bolt of lightning, knocking a lump of stone from its shoulder and prompting concerns that the Admiral's one remaining (left) arm might drop off. To prevent this from happening, a bronze 'bandage' was put in place.

In 1925, a Scottish confidence trickster cheekily 'sold' the monument to an American for £6,000. He is also thought to have secured £1,000 from someone keen to acquire the tower known as Big Ben.

Adolf Hitler also liked the column, in particular for what it represented, and reportedly planned to take it back to Berlin following the successful invasion of Britain. (The Nazis wanted Cleopatra's Needle, too, although the reasons for this are not known.)

WELLINGTON FINALLY MEETS HIS WATERLOO

The Duke of Wellington is the only non-Royal to have two statues in London showing him mounted on a horse, but in fact there should have been three. The third and largest was so large – more than 30 ft tall – that its construction required more than 40 tons of captured French cannon to be melted down to provide the bronze.

Unfortunately, it was so ugly that, on seeing it, a Frenchman is said to have proclaimed '*Nous somme vengés . . .*' – we are avenged.[1] Londoners, too, were quick to demand the eyesore be got rid of, and Queen Victoria apparently agreed – not least because Wellington was shown seated on the wrong horse – but insisted that the removal be delayed until Wellington had died. The figure is now positioned in Surrey.

Monuments That Aren't Quite What They Seem

One of London's most famous monuments – **Eros** in Piccadilly Circus – actually depicts Anteros, the Greek god of requited love, although most tourists assume it is the Roman god Cupid.

1 In London at least, Napoleon Bonaparte arguably fared no better. His own statue, showing him completely naked for extra humiliation, still stands at the foot of the stairs of Apsley House, the London home of his nemesis, the Iron Duke.

The statue of **Oliver Cromwell** outside Westminster Hall shows him wearing his spurs upside-down, although it is not known whether this is an error on the part of the artist or a calculated insult.

If the paws on the **Trafalgar Square lions** look a little odd, it is because sculptor Edwin Landseer modelled them on those of a domestic cat after the lion's corpse he had been working from finally began to fester and had to be abandoned.

G. F. Handel had such weird ears – at least according to Louis-François Roubillac – that when carving the composer's likeness for Westminster Abbey, the Frenchman found it more acceptable to copy those of a young woman he knew.

St Pancras New Church on the Euston Road was inspired by two highly influential buildings in Athens – the Erechtheum and the Tower of the Winds. Unfortunately, the Greek Revival caryatids placed outside it were sculpted to the wrong scale so that the young ladies had later to have several inches removed from above their waists in order to fit the finished building.

The statue outside St Thomas's Hospital of Britain's most famous nurse, **Florence Nightingale,** is a fibreglass copy of the original, which was stolen in 1970 and never recovered.

Also lost are the original genitalia of the **South Bank Lion** outside County Hall. The lion originally stood on top of a brewery further along the bank, presumably too high to cause offence, but the ensemble was considered a tad lewd when he was installed on a lower plinth and steps were taken to emasculate the poor beast.

A similar fate was meted out to the figures on the façade of what is now the **Embassy of Zimbabwe** on the Strand. Carved by Jacob

Epstein, 'The Ages of Man' caused such a scandal in Edwardian England that certain specifically masculine portions of the figures were cut back following the public outcry about their dimensions. (Similar complaints about his work at 55 Broadway, the headquarters of what became London Underground, led to the penises of 'Night' and 'Day' being shortened by 1½ in.)

In the **Henry VII Chapel** at Westminster Abbey, a carving of St Matthew shows the apostle wearing a pair of spectacles, although these were not invented until at least 1,200 years after his death.

While it is the Monument in Fish Street Hill that officially commemorates the Great Fire of London, the rebuilt **St Paul's** is, for many visitors, the definitive reminder of that time. But how many of them realise, however, that the gilded flames above the dome incline in such a way as to indicate the direction of the wind on the first day of the fire in 1666?

The sixteenth-century statue inside the gates of **St Dunstan-in-the-West** in Fleet Street is the only statue of Elizabeth I anywhere in London. Were this not in itself surprising enough, for such a popular sovereign, it was lost for many years when for reasons now forgotten it was deposited in the cellar of a local pub. London's third-oldest statue (see below), it was discovered only by accident, by workmen demolishing the building in 1839, after which it was put back on display.

London's Oldest Statue

The title is usually awarded to a badly weathered statue standing in the middle of Southwark's beautifully unspoiled Trinity Church Square. This is popularly supposed to be of King Alfred, but no one knows for sure. At barely 600 years old, however, it postdates its subject by several centuries and is therefore nowhere near as ancient as the black basalt bust situated over the main entrance to Sotheby's Bond Street headquarters.

The bust in question is of an Egyptian lion god, Sekhmet, and was auctioned in the early nineteenth century but never collected by the buyer. Eventually, Sotheby's adopted it as the company's unofficial mascot, and it has since been dated to approximately 1320 BC.

Ten Blue Plaques Not Yet Awarded

Saracen's Head Buildings, Cock Lane, EC1

The London showroom of John J. Royle, Mancunian inventor of the world's first self-pouring teapot (Patent no. 6327, dated 1886).

Wood Green Empire, High Street, N22

In March 1918, the Chinese magician Chung Ling Soo (real name Bill Robinson) dropped down dead here after failing to catch a bullet in his teeth, during the death-defying finale to his famous stage show. Although it turned out to be less death-defying than he'd have planned.

68 Tottenham Court Road, W1

Where an unknown John Lydon (Johnny Rotten) was briefly employed handing out leaflets on behalf of the Official Church of Scientology. Usually, of course, it's the other way round and celebrities wait until they've made it before coming to the cult.

81–82 Pall Mall, SW1

Where the notorious eighteenth-century quack Dr James Graham established his Temple of Health & Hymen. With its mirrored ceiling, giant bed and rather worrying-sounding 'medico-Electrical apparatus', childless couples were invited to attend and to 'obtain the desire of their lives'. Graham made a mint selling his unfortunate gulls 'imperial pills, electrical aether and nervous aethereal balsoms', but then found religion and died in an asylum.

34 Haydock Green, Northolt, Middlesex

Stanley Green died here in 1994 after spending more than twenty-five years walking up and down Oxford Street carrying a placard warning shoppers of the perils of protein. (The placard – 'Less Lust, By Less Protein' – is now in the Museum of London.)

18 St James's Square, SW1

Home to the only suicide buried in Westminster Abbey. In 1822, Foreign Secretary Lord Castlereagh killed himself with a pocket knife, but was afforded the honour even though committing suicide was a serious crime (and remained so until 1961). The public were outraged, rioted outside the house and booed Castlereagh's coffin when it appeared.

Church House, Great Smith Street, SW1

Self-proclaimed prophet Joanna Southcott left a locked box here, insisting it be opened only after her death and with twenty-four bishops as witnesses. She died in 1814 – without giving birth to the new Messiah, as she had promised to do – and when the box was opened it contained nothing more than a few coins, a night-cap and a trashy novel.

Leicester Square Theatre, WC2

Built on the site of Lucy's Bagnio – essentially a brothel – where in 1762 an illiterate Surrey woman Mary Tofts claimed to have given birth to fifteen rabbits. Several surgeons appeared to believe her – including George I's personal physician – but she was threatened with prosecution under a medieval statute as a 'vile cheat and imposter'. The charge refused to stick, however – the hoaxed realising they would look pretty foolish in court – and she returned to Surrey and resumed a life of petty crime.

201 Deptford High Street, SE8

After breaking a German spy ring operating from this address in 1915, British Intelligence continued supplying information to the enemy – all of it false – while invoicing them for the service at a rate of £6 a week.

71 Brewer Street, W1

Marks the site of the home for thirty-three years of the diplomat, soldier and spy Chevalier Charles d'Eon de Beaumont (1728–1810). In the 1770s, the Chevalier began dressing as a woman, scandalising London society and encouraging more than £100,000-worth of wagers about his sexuality. A jury eventually ruled that the Chevalier was indeed a woman but, before interment at St Pancras Old Church, doctors determined that the body was anatomically that of a man.

If You Want to Get Ahead, Get a . . . Beaver

High above busy Oxford Street – on the roof of numbers 105–9 – are three of London's strangest little statues. If anyone noticed them from the pavement they could be rats, but on closer inspection they turn out to be beavers, the wide flat tail of one of them being just about visible from the street. It's a curious choice – an animal that is no longer either native or much loved and not especially heroic – but the rear of the building provides a clue. Here, large terracotta letters in relief spell out the words 'HAT FACTORY – HENRY HEATH – OXFORD STREET'.

From the 1820s until the 1930s, the factory annually turned out thousands of top hats and others, the buyers of which were promised 'First, Their Quality; Second, Excellence of Finish; Third, Style'. Traditionally, such hats were made using felted fur from 'Beaver, Otter, Rabbits, Hares and Musk Rats', the first of these being much preferred as it offered better protection against the English rain.

In part because of this quality, the European beaver had been hunted to extinction long before 1820, but quantities of Canadian beaver were imported by the Hudson's Bay Company from the 1700s onwards and London hatters used it wherever possible.

Acknowledging the animals' contribution, Mr Heath incorporated three of them into this charming building's design – unfortunately so high up that passers-by rarely notice them – and in St Helen's Place, Bishopsgate, another can be seen on the gilded weathervane of what was once the London headquarters of the Hudson's Bay Company itself.

7
Dead London

'Do you realise that people die of boredom in London suburbs? It's the second biggest cause of death amongst the English in general. Sheer boredom . . .'

Alexander McCall Smith

LONDON'S WEIRDEST WILLS

A. A. Milne

J. M. Barrie famously bequeathed the rights to *Peter Pan* to Great Ormond Street Hospital for Sick Children – which kind of makes sense. When it came to disposing of the rights to *Winnie the Pooh*, however, A. A. Milne curiously decided to divide the profits between his wife and son (that is, Christopher Robin and his mother), his *alma mater* Westminster School, and the already well-upholstered Garrick Club in Covent Garden.

As recently as 1998, the club's fortunate members were still wondering what to do with all the cash pouring in from Disney. Depressingly, several wished to divide the massive honeypot among themselves – a windfall of nearly £40,000 each, apparently – but in the end it was decided to refurbish the clubhouse and then to give anything left over to charity.

Jeremy Bentham

The eighteenth-century philosopher (and founder of University College London) firmly believed that the bodies of dead people should be put to more practical use than being simply stuck in the ground. In particular, he felt that great men should be preserved and put on display to encourage others to excel.

If properly preserved, his Will insisted, every man could be reborn as his own statue. Accordingly, when he died in 1832, he had himself dissected, embalmed, stuffed and mounted in a smart glass case by the entrance to UCL. It's still there today but sadly now has a wax head, as the original rotted away.

Charles II

Royal Wills traditionally remain hidden from view but fortunately the odd, impetuous monarch cannot help but betray his true feelings – and so it was with Charles II. While apologising for taking so long to die, he asked his brother (James II) to 'let not poor Nelly starve' – and Nell Gwynn never did.

Besides securing the prestigious Dukedom of St Albans for her illegitimate son (fathered by Charles), Nell also got a splendid address for herself: 79 Pall Mall. More than 300 years later, the house Nell knew has gone, but its replacement is still the only freehold property on the south side of the street, with the remainder held by the Crown.

Ben Jonson

The actor and dramatist Ben Jonson (1572–1637) managed to grab one of the much-prized plots close to Poets' Corner in Westminster Abbey – plenty of eminent men and women apply but fail to get one – but, bizarrely, his Will led to him being buried standing up.

This was almost certainly because Jonson's reduced circumstances meant he could not afford a larger plot than one 18 in. square. For much the same reason, the inscription on his tomb spells his name incorrectly – 'Johnson' – almost certainly because the same Will allowed just 18*d* (or 7½p) for the inscription, which even back then paid for only the lowest class of stonemason.

William Somerset Maugham

One of the most prolific, best-selling, widely read and wealthiest authors of the twentieth century, Somerset Maugham was briefly married, lived at 6 Chesterfield Gardens, Mayfair, and had a family. He nevertheless changed his Will to leave his fortune to a young man from the slums of Bermondsey, doing so while very publicly disowning his daughter Liza.

She contested the amendments to the Will, and these were eventually overturned. But Maugham's response was vicious and, in a new volume of memoirs, he revealed that his daughter had been born out of wedlock. This came as a shock to Liza and to polite society in London and alienated many of the author's fans and oldest friends.

London's Magnificent Seven

People are living longer, the mortality rate in the capital is at its lowest ever, and cremation has never been more popular than now. But even with an estimated 70 per cent of people opting for cremation, 50,000 deaths a year in London mean more than five acres of fresh ground have to be found each year to bury them. Moreover, the problem is getting worse, with many recent arrivals, including Muslims, Buddhists and Orthodox Christians, showing a religious preference for inhumation.

Of course, the capital has always been massively overcrowded, and not just for the living. The search for burial space is a long-standing problem – recall Samuel Pepys bribing a sexton in Chapter 5 – and some of the solutions have been truly gruesome. At nineteenth-century Spa Fields in Islington, for example, an estimated 80,000 bodies were squeezed into space intended for 1,000 by mutilating remains and burning their coffins.

To avoid such horrors, most Londoners now – and indeed for several generations – have been buried many miles from where they lived. This is chiefly because all the inner London boroughs long ago ran out of space and very few churchyards – and none at all near the centre – have even a single vacant plot.

The decisive change was back in the mid-nineteenth century, with the creation of the so-called Victorian Valhallas, a series of vast and often beautifully landscaped cemeteries. These were well away from the city's historic centre and expressly devised to accommodate its growing population of dead.

By far the largest is East Finchley's St Pancras and Islington Cemetery where more than 800,000 burials have been conducted, on a site extending over 190 acres. (The famous London Necropolis covers an area ten times the size, and was once connected to Waterloo by its own private railway; but this is well outside London, at Brookwood in Surrey, and anyway has only a quarter as many graves.)

The most celebrated, however, are the Magnificent Seven, the creation of which was encouraged by an Act of Parliament brought in during a rapid period of growth during the first half of the nineteenth century. This saw the population of London more than double from around one million to well over two, and with parish churchyards literally overflowing – as unsightly and distressing for the living as it was dangerous – traditional parish burials were no longer possible, even for the very rich.

In the face of the crisis, many solutions were proposed, perhaps the strangest of which was the construction of an immense, ninety-four-storey pyramid on Primrose Hill. Large enough to dwarf anything the pharaohs had commissioned, and with room inside for an incredible 5,167,104 of London's dead, Thomas Willson's Brobdingnagian scheme was eventually shelved in favour of a simple plan to remove the deceased to what the 1830 Act called 'places where they would be less prejudicial to the health of the inhabitants.'

The idea immediately proved both popular and fashionable, in large part because young, hungry and energetic joint-stock entrepreneurs embraced it with enormous enthusiasm. Entities such as the newly formed General Cemetery Company and the splendidly named London Necropolis and National Mausoleum Company identified at once an opportunity for great profit in the provision of beautiful, Elysian landscapes in which to accommodate the monied dead and their families.

1832 – Kensal Green Cemetery

At Kensal Green, the first of these companies planted many hundreds of trees on its new 54-acre site, while a stylish Greek Revival chapel was even equipped with such mod cons as hydraulic lifts to take the deceased down into the spacious and beautifully appointed catacombs below.

Once the cemetery had bagged its first two Royal Highnesses – younger children of George III – London's rich and fashionable quickly followed. Today, visitors wandering through what has often been described as the 'Belgravia of Death' can find many famous names, including those of Thackeray, Trollope and Wilkie Collins, Sir Marc and Isambard Kingdom Brunel, and Victorian England's leading showman Blondin, who crossed the Niagara on a tightrope before retiring to Ealing. W. H. Smith is another guest, whose tomb takes the form of a massive stone book, and General James Barry who, on his death in 1865, was discovered to have been a woman.

1837 – West Norwood Cemetery

Smaller but no less spectacular – it has around seventy Grade II and II* listed buildings and monuments – West Norwood has seen around 200,000 burials and cremations with many thousands more interred in a massive series of catacombs and the fabulous Greek Orthodox Necropolis.

The cookery writer Mrs Beeton is buried here in a very simple tomb (she was only 28), as is the machine-gun pioneer Sir Hiram Maxim. Anyone in search of something more extravagant can do no better than seek out the family vault designed for Sir Henry Doulton – of Royal Doulton fame – which is created almost entirely of pottery and terracotta.

1839 – Highgate Cemetery

The famous final resting place of Karl Marx, an active body of supporters means that Highgate is now perhaps the best preserved cemetery in London. With an abundance of Egyptian architectural features – as previously noted, the 'style of the Nile' was much in vogue at the time of its creation – it boasts three large Grade I structures and is an important wildlife reserve for this part of London. The most eccentric monument, however, was designed for the Maples furniture-store family and resembles a vast four-poster bed.

As the cemetery is still open for business, the 170,000 residents are a nicely varied bunch and, as well as the usual Victorian grandees, they include author Douglas Adams, Lucien Freud, and the father of current Labour leader Ed Milliband. The latter was a communist like Marx, yet both ended up in a place famous for maintaining rigid class distinctions and for pricing plots at a level calculated to ensure that none of the 'workers of the world' could even consider moving in alongside them.

1840 – Abney Park Cemetery

Creating Europe's first wholly non-denominational 'burial garden', the creators of Abney Park in East London also favoured Egyptian motifs, in part as a way to avoid reliance on conventional religious iconography.

The architect was an engineering professor called William Hosking (who curiously preferred to be buried at Highgate) and its chief glory is perhaps the trees, more than 2,500 of them on 32 acres. These make it a hugely atmospheric place but also harder to navigate even though the species were planted in alphabetical order, from *Acer* to *Zanthoxylum*.

Religious dissenters naturally make up much of the population, including Salvation Army founders William and Catherine Booth, the abolitionist preacher Dr Thomas Binney, and the Chartist leader James O'Brien. It was also used for the video of *Back to Black* by singer Amy Winehouse, although she is not buried here but in Edgware, north London.

In 2012, the composer Benjamin Till wrote *The London Requiem* after researching 20,000 epitaphs on graves in various of the capital's cemeteries. With contributions from actors Barbara Windsor and Matt Lucas, the playwright Sir Arnold Wesker and singers Tanita Tikaram and Maddie Prior, the finished work was first performed at Abney Park.

ROCK OF AGES

Like the wildly varied composition of the Albert Memorial,[1] London's great cemeteries can make amateur geologists of us all as one attempts to follow the changing fashions in Victorian England, first for this stone then for that. Most obviously, it was the growth of the railways that made it possible to bring such heavy material into the capital from remote areas further afield, and, over time, London's more traditional Bath and Portland stone monuments gave way to some fairly exotic alternatives.

Granite was particularly popular as it was expensive to work but very durable and could be highly polished. It also offered consumers a very wide palette of different colours, such as pink stone from the Peterhead quarries near Aberdeen and from Ross and Mull, grey peppered stone from Bodmin, and a reddish Shap granite from Cumbria that sparkled with tiny feldspar crystals. White Carrara marble was imported from Italy at even greater expense, but its relative softness lent itself to the kind of elaborate figurative carving the Victorians liked. That said, even now, more than a century later, it still looks slightly alien in a London setting.

1 The Albert Memorial is particularly good in this regard. It includes granite from the Mountains of Mourne, Cornwall and Mull, Welsh slate, Blue John from the Peak District, new red sandstone, the inevitable Portland stone in various different shades, Carrara marble for the famous friezes, and numerous fossils in its Derbyshire stone paving slabs.

1840 – Brompton Cemetery

The most central of the seven, and a generous patch of green space in this part of the royal borough, the cemetery has seen more than 200,000 interments and, after a long period of closure, is once again open for business. Despite a number of high-profile burials, the most popular headstones for modern grave-spotters seem to be those of Messrs. Nutkins, McGregor and Tod, three otherwise undistinguished Londoners whose names – together with those of fellow cemetery residents Jeremiah Fisher, Tommy Brock and Peter Rabbett (sic) – were borrowed by Beatrix Potter who, for nearly fifty years, lived nearby at 2 Bolton Gardens.

1840 – Nunhead Cemetery

Despite the magnificent vista from the North Gate entrance to Thomas Little's octagonal Anglican Chapel, this is very much the poor relation of the seven although, after years of neglect – and the destruction by vandals of many important monuments – the cemetery has now been restored and reopened. It is today a wonderful, ivy-draped Gothic landscape, full of atmosphere and carved angels, and rich in symbolic reminders of the Victorians' near obsession with the furniture of death.

There are, for example, dozens of broken columns and inverted torches, both emblems signifying lives cut short, while on the main gate piers representations of the Egyptian ouroboros – a snake swallowing its tail – conversely hint at the eternity of existence. Draped urns similarly indicate that the deceased was the master of his house, while weeping angels provide an echo of ancient times when the living would have been paid to stand and weep beside the tombs of the rich. Stepped monuments are a subtle reminder of the departing soul's three steps to Heaven, and traditional trefoil designs a more obvious reference to the Holy Trinity.

1841 – Tower Hamlets Cemetery

With more than 350,000 burials, Tower Hamlets has by far the largest proportion of so-called public graves, ones set aside for those who could not afford any kind of funeral. Within ten years of its opening, these accounted for four-fifths of burials here, the plots remaining the property of the cemetery company amidst rumours that paupers were being buried up to 40 ft deep and with thirty to a grave.

If nothing else, the thought is a chilling reminder of the reality of life and death in the Victorian East End, and it was perhaps inevitable that eventually the cemetery would be taken into public ownership when its commercial viability faltered for want of a better-heeled clientele. Vandals, neglect and wartime bombing have since taken a dreadful toll on both its chapels – Early English for the Anglicans, Byzantine for the non-conformists – and, sadly, on most of the memorials as well. Today, it is a melancholy place, and not in a good way.

NOT QUITE DEAD

Londoners (real and honorary) who got to read their own obituaries:

Mark Twain

A resident of Tedworth Square, Chelsea, during which time he accompanied the Prince of Wales on the first ever Central Line train journey, author Mark Twain – real name Samuel Clemens – was twice confronted by his own mortality. Consequently, he is as famous now for his quip that any reports of his death were an exaggeration as for any line in *The Adventures of Huckleberry Finn* or *The Adventures of Tom Sawyer.*

The confusion first arose in 1897 when a journalist enquired after his health. In fact, it was his cousin who was dangerously ill. Twain recounted the incident in an edition of the *New York Journal* and used that celebrated, much quoted line. In the event, he lived another thirteen years, eventually dying at the age of seventy-four in Redding, Connecticut.

Alice Cooper

As long as there has been pop, its stars have upheld the tradition of dying young, and in the 1970s Cooper must have looked like a prime candidate. It was therefore more in sadness than surprise that a report of his death was published by the music newspaper *Melody Maker* from its Stamford Street office overlooking the Thames.

In fact, the whole thing was meant to be a joke, a mock obituary written as a satirical comment on one of Cooper's less successful concerts. Thousands of fans fell for it, however, but were soon to receive reassurance from an official statement from the singer stating categorically that he was 'alive, and drunk as usual'.

Alan Whicker

Even worse than reading you are dead must be reading that you never amounted to much anyway. Such was the fate of Richmond resident Alan Whicker who, in conversation with Michael Parkinson, told how during the Korean War he had been reported 'killed in action' while flying with the Army behind enemy lines.

The report confused Whicker's little Piper Cub with one that had crashed to the ground nearby. Telling Parky about it years later, he was pretty matter-of-fact, saying, '"Alan Whicker, war correspondent of *Exchange*

Telegraph, unfortunately was shot down . . ." And then a little bit about my lack of achievement.'

Paul McCartney

The fact that his simple lack of shoes on the cover of *Abbey Road* was enough to convince the faithful that Macca was dead is perhaps less surprising when one learns that rumours about his death had been circulating long before the album was released in 1969.

In fact, the first seems to have surfaced three years earlier in a call to WKNR-FM radio in Detroit. This was picked up by a New York station shortly afterwards, and although the DJ was promptly fired, the rumour sparked several theories that John, George and Ringo had already hired a lookalike to fill the gap.

Ian Dury

In 1998, Bob Geldof hosted a radio show on Xfm and was tipped for a Sony award despite being described by the *NME* as 'the world's worst DJ'. In particular, the paper was unimpressed with the way he had announced Dury's death live on air – well over a year before the veteran rocker finally passed on.

The cause is thought to have been an ill-informed call from a listener, as Dury was ill at the time and had been diagnosed with cancer. However, he continued performing into 2000, although for his last performance (at the London Palladium) he had had to be helped on to and off the stage.

Dave Swarbrick

In April 1999, the *Daily Telegraph* published an obituary after the New Malden-born folk musician and Fairport

Convention stalwart was admitted to hospital in the Midlands with a serious chest infection. Lengthy and full of praise for the singer-songwriter's talents, it was nevertheless highly premature as 'Swarb' continues regularly to gig well over a decade later.

It must have been a shock – before a double lung transplant he had a history of chest problems, and was confined to a wheelchair – but the performer rose to the occasion and was reported by the BBC as having noted, 'It's not the first time I have died in Coventry.'

Ernest Hemingway

The author met his fourth and final wife in London, and although he was destined to die by his own hand in 1961, the pair were involved in numerous car, ski and 'plane crashes in the early 1950s. In one of the latter, Hemingway sustained a serious head injury, and was reported dead by several US newspapers.

Never quite recovering, his injuries affected him for the rest of his life, and his drinking, already heavy, intensified as he fought the pain. Hemingway remained haunted by the incidents and reportedly read a scrapbook containing the obituaries every morning whilst drinking a glass of champagne.

Last Word – London Epitaphs

'Sacred to the Memory of Major James Brush who was killed by the accidental discharge of a pistol by his orderly 14th April 1831 – Well done, o good and faithful servant.'

St Mary Magdalene, Woolwich.

'Aged 207 years. Holywell Street. Thomas Cam.'

Burial Register, St Leonard's, Shoreditch.

'Tho: Parr Of Ye County Of Sallop. Borne In Ad: 1483. He Lived In Ye Reignes Of Ten Princes Viz: K.Edw.4. K.Ed.5. K.Rich.3. K.Hen.7. K.Hen.8. K.Edw.6. Q.Ma. Q.Eliz. K.Ja. & K.Charles. Aged 152 Yeares & Was Buryed Here Novemb. 15 1635.'

Westminster Abbey.

'Here lyeth wrapped in clay The body of Wiliam Wray. I have no more to say.'

St Michael's, Crooked Lane, City of London.

'Exit Burbage, 1619.'

St Leonard's, Shoreditch.

8

Royal London

'Like all the best families, we have our share of eccentricities, of impetuous and wayward youngsters and of family disagreements.'

HM Queen Elizabeth II

What They Do When They're Not Being Royal

HM The Queen

Besides her famous corgis and dorgis, the Queen is a keen pigeon fancier in her spare time, with more than 250 birds of her own. Each has a leg ring, clearly marked with the royal monogram 'ER', but sadly this was not enough to prevent one of Her Majesty's favourites being attacked and eaten by a sparrowhawk during training for the 2005 St Malo to Malvern race.

Like her late sister Princess Margaret (who, on several occasions, won small prizes in regular competitions set by the magazine *Country Life*), the Queen likes doing crosswords and jigsaw puzzles. She is also a fan of the Beatles' film *Yellow*

Submarine, which she saw four times when it first opened, and likes to wash up once a year following a family barbecue at Balmoral.

Most unroyal moment: being ticked off by her own sister who, on being told to behave herself, replied, 'You look after your Empire, and I'll look after my life.'

HRH The Duke of Edinburgh

Horse racing might be the sport of kings but, unlike his wife, daughter-in-law and late mother-in-law, the Duke of Edinburgh has always preferred cricket. Because of this, he has been known to wear a special top hat to the racecourse, one equipped with a concealed radio receiver enabling him to keep up with the score.

As well as sporting an uncharacteristically trendy black suede dinner jacket in the 1960s (and, on one occasion, jeans with the price tag still attached), the Duke of Edinburgh conceived a passion for cooking his own sausages at the breakfast table. Eventually he had to stop, however, when the Queen took exception to the smell permeating through the Palace.

On marrying, he also gave up cigarettes.

Most unroyal moment: being voted 'Best Dictator for Britain' ahead of Enoch Powell and Harold Wilson in a poll of *Daily Telegraph* readers, and asking a Scottish driving instructor, 'How do you keep the natives off the booze long enough to pass the test?'

HM George VI

The Queen's father was known to enjoy running the projector backwards when he watched home cine films. Apparently, he found it particularly funny when the film included swimmers exiting the pool feet first and ending up on the diving board. (The sight of pigs walking backwards is also funnier than you might think.)

George VI was also the first reigning monarch to watch a

motor race – the 1950 British Grand Prix at Silverstone – but generally preferred quieter pursuits and did not repeat the experience. Skilled at embroidery, he presented his wife with a dozen petit-point chair covers for her to use at Royal Lodge Windsor, and, like William IV, George IV and Edward VII – and indeed his brother, Edward VIII – he was an active freemason.

Most unroyal moment: in 1945, His Majesty asked President Truman for his autograph.

HM Edward VII

Queen Victoria's eldest son so enjoyed watching buildings on fire that he ordered his own fireman's uniforms so he could do it *incognito.* These were kept at Chandos Street in the West End, and Watling Street in the City, and, afterwards, he liked to go for a plate of tripe in Tottenham Court Road.

An enthusiastic ten-pin bowler and a fine shot (he had a lane installed at Sandringham, and the world's largest game larder), Edward was also a big fan of snowball fights. Never shy of stealing the royal advantage, he would insist that guests at his Norfolk estate stand stock still while he and his children pelted them with snowballs.

Most unroyal moment: being besieged by moneylenders at a hotel in Paris when a newspaper revealed the true extent of his debts.

HM Edward VIII

A lifetime sucker for funny accents, as Prince of Wales Edward VIII routinely spoke a kind of mockney so that he pronounced the word 'lady' to rhyme with 'tidy'. Knowing this annoyed his father enormously, he also adopted his American wife's pronunciation to become the 'Dook' of Windsor and referred to children as 'kids' throughout his book, *A Family Album.*

Edward was also unusually musical for a member of the Royal Family, but had a habit of picking instruments that annoy a lot of people such as the banjo, bagpipes and ukelele. It was also his habit of wearing a grey top hat rather than a black one that set the fashion for Ascot that still persists.

Most unroyal moment: His Royal Highness used ungrammatically to invite friends to accompany 'the Duchess and I' after his abdication, and was once heard telling the conductor to 'Hurry it up, man' during a performance of the 'National Anthem'.

HM Queen Victoria

Queen Victoria was a demon card-player, as good at it as she was keen, and insisted that anyone who lost a hand to her settle their debts immediately. Because she would accept only newly minted coins for this, her tendency to win meant a ready supply of new money had to be kept at the Palace at all times.

At least prior to her widowhood, Her Majesty was also a keen traveller and would take tiny marble carvings of her many children's hands wherever she went. The Queen commissioned a similar sculpture of her beloved Prince Albert's 'sweet little ear', and following his early death made sure that this much treasured keepsake was always close at hand.

Most unroyal moment: being caught drawing her royal cipher 'VRI' on dusty furniture at Windsor Castle, and having her claret pepped up with whisky.

HRH The Prince of Wales

Once a small boy like any other, Prince Charles amassed quite a collection of cheap plastic models from cereal packets. He would reportedly get jolly upset if the staff at Buckingham Palace refused to open a new box of cereal – so he could have the toy immediately – before the contents of the last one had been finished.

Later in life, he acquired two miniature chastity belts and a considerable number of toy trolls of the sort that were fashionable among children in the 1960s. In London, these were arranged on the chimneypieces of his various private apartments, but his first wife Diana did not share his enthusiasm for them and they were packed away following their marriage.

HM George V

Even his official biographer admitted that, though a wise old king, George V 'did nothing at all but kill animals and stick in stamps' – but of the latter he was a shrewd collector who bought extremely well. Now owned by the Queen, his 325 albums are thought to comprise the most valuable collection of their kind in the world.

In 1904, Sir Arthur Davidson, variously equerry to Victoria, Edward VII and George, telephoned the king to tell him that some 'damned fool has given as much as £1,400 for a single stamp'. Equivalent to more than £125,000 in today's money, the king hung up after telling Davidson 'that damned fool was me'.

Most unroyal moment: falling through the wicker seat of a chair as he was about to make his Christmas broadcast to the nation, and having 'Daisy, Daisy (A Bicycle Built for Two)' played at his wedding.

HM Queen Mary

The wife of George V collected many things, more than a few of them from the homes of friends. Not exactly light-fingered, and far too well mannered to ask for something outright, she would tell her hostess how much she liked something in the knowledge that her reputation would have preceded her and they would almost certainly take the hint.

Bizarrely for such a self-consciously grande dame, Mary

learned the words to 'Yes, We Have No Bananas' and was another one who had a brief flirtation with speaking mockney. Meeting Stanley Baldwin during Edward VIII's abdication crisis, she told the Prime Minister, 'Well, really, Mr Baldwin – this is a pretty kettle of fish!' In fact, she was appalled by her son's actions and is thought to have lost 25 lb before the crisis was resolved.

Most unroyal moment: prior to her marriage to the future king, family debts meant Mary and her parents had to live abroad for an extended period as an economy measure.

HM Queen Elizabeth the Queen Mother

Unlike her daughter, who learned to strip and service an engine during a spell with the wartime Auxiliary Territorial Service, Queen Elizabeth the Queen Mother never set out to be the practical sort. She nevertheless amassed a surprising array of skills and, an expert fly-fisher, would routinely land 20-lb fish when staying at her castle on the coast of Caithness.

She could also play the bongos, a skill she demonstrated in 1974, and on a visit to the London Press Club showed herself to be equally adept at billiards. Finally, she proved to be a convincing big-game hunter and once successfully dropped a charging rhino with a single shot from a .275-calibre rifle.

Most unroyal moment: possibly midday. According to a report in the *Guardian*, the Queen Mother typically drank 70 units of alcohol every week, starting with a daily gin and Dubonnet at noon. She died aged 101.

9

Shopping London

'The young Japanese, especially, love to wear the latest thing and when they come to London they head for my shops as part of what they want to find in Britain.'

Vivienne Westwood

Respect Where It's Warranted

It's not all Crown Jewels, caviar and champagne, but for visitors to London, keen to shop where the top people shop, a Royal Warrant in the window of a shop or business has long been taken as a reliable guide for anyone seeking prestige brands and the most upmarket retailers.

For literally centuries, royal patronage has exercised an understandably powerful influence on a wide variety of trades and craftsmen, and even in an age of celebrity endorsement the favour of official royal recognition – that all-important phrase, 'By Appointment to' – is still regarded as a uniquely important honour by those granted permission to use it.

Successful merchants in medieval London already enjoyed formal links with the Crown by means of Royal Charters granted to the various Guilds or Livery Companies.[1] The first such was given by Henry II to the Weavers Company in 1155. As trade expanded under the Tudors and Stuarts, so these grants increased, typically in the form of so-called Letters Patent, until the reign of Queen Victoria when the accepted instrument of preferment became the same Royal Warrant of Appointment that is in use today.

As such an obvious privilege and a much sought-after accolade, its use has naturally been carefully governed over that time by a number of strict regulations. These are designed principally to emphasise its value and prestige, but also to ward off fakers and fraudsters and – as a consequence – to ensure that today's 800 or so Royal Warrant holders fully deserve the status they enjoy as suppliers to one of the three senior Royals.

HARRODS V SELFRIDGES[2]

Harrods

In 1898 installs the first escalator in England, with attendants dispensing brandy and Epsom Salts to customers traumatised after trying it out for the first time.

Selfridges

In 1910 becomes the first store anywhere in the world to have a ground-floor beauty hall – one that is still the world's largest, and that has been copied by virtually every department store the world over.

1 See list of Livery Companies in Chapter 13.

2 Both stores originally included a grammatically precise apostrophe in their names, but Harrod's abandoned this in 1921 and Selfridge's in 1940.

Harrods

Uses 12,000 light bulbs to illuminate the famous façade of the store. Around 300 need replacing every day.

Selfridges

Used 30,000 light bulbs to illuminate its façade as part of its twentieth anniversary celebrations, but perhaps sensibly decides to take them down afterwards.

Harrods

Once sold a skunk intended for the purchaser's ex-wife, and an elephant for future US president Ronald Reagan.

Selfridges

Employed John Logie Baird to demonstrate his new invention, the 'televisor'. (Fast forward to today and its Knightsbridge rival has a 152-in. flat-screen Panasonic model on display, yours for an eye-watering £600,000.)

Harrods

Supplied A. A. Milne with the toy bear that was to inspire the creation of *Winnie the Pooh* (see Chapter 10 – Green London – for more on the bear).

Selfridges

Commissioned the world's longest and largest ever photograph. At nearly 1,000 ft long, Sam Taylor-Wood's modern interpretation of the Parthenon frieze was used to conceal the scaffolding during work on the store's façade in 2000.

Harrods

In 2011, the store was offering a 'diamond manicure' for £32,000.

Selfridges

After the first cross-Channel flight in 1909, thousands queued all night to see Louis Blériot's monoplane, which was exhibited in the store.

Harrods

Official motto is *omnia omnibus ubique* – 'All things for all people, everywhere'.

Selfridges

Founder Harry Gordon Selfridge coined the phrases 'The customer is never wrong' and 'Only xx shopping days to Christmas'.

As in the Middle Ages, the junior Royals do not enjoy the right to grant such Warrants. Previous grantors have included Queen Elizabeth the Queen Mother, for example, but not Diana, Princess of Wales. Prince William is similarly not entitled to grant Warrants of his own.[3] Instead, only regular suppliers to

---

3 Interestingly, as the Diamond Jubilee Year drew to its conclusion, it was announced that London's Goring Hotel was to receive a Royal Warrant 'for Hospitality Services', and the connection was clearly the Prince's. The hotel was, of course, where Catherine Middleton spent the night before her wedding, but the grantor was HM The Queen.

the Queen, Prince Philip and the Prince of Wales are entitled to display the relevant Royal Arms at their place of business, as well as on company stationery.

While explicitly not intended to give particular manufacturers or retailers what might be considered a right royal advantage, they have always done so. The same strict rules govern the display of the Royal Arms on any products offered for sale, and on the packaging of these products, but even with these restrictions in place a Royal Warrant can serve as the best possible advertisement for any business – and this has long been recognised.

As long ago as 1684, an official history by Edward Chamberlayne, Doctor at Law, conceded that suppliers of goods to St James's Palace and other royal homes were 'offices and places of good credit, great profit and enjoyed by Persons of Quality'. Similarly now, more than 300 years later, and presumably in the belief that if it's good enough for Her Majesty it's good enough for them, many shoppers from both home and abroad still delight in making a small royal connection whenever they reach for their wallet.

In order to qualify for a Royal Warrant of Appointment, a company must have 'made a supply or provided a service for a department of the Royal Household in respect of any of the Royal Residences, official or private'. This supply or service should have covered a period of not less than five years and 'the quantity must be in reasonable proportion to the whole of that type of goods or service used' by the Royal Household concerned.

Providing these criteria are met, a Warrant is initially granted for a period of ten years, after which time it is reviewed by the Lord Chamberlain's Office. Naturally, it can also be cancelled at any time during that period should the rules be flouted. (Or, for that matter, if the grantor changes his mind, as the Duke of Edinburgh decided to do in 2000 when Harrods owner Mohammed Al Fayed made some quite extraordinary accusations against the Prince. Al Fayed's response was even more bizarre – he called in the press and publicly burned all four of his warrants.)

The regulations state, too, that Her Majesty and the two Royal Dukes can each grant only one Warrant to any single business, but that a company can hold Warrants from more than one Member of the Royal Family. Over the years, a favoured few have held as many as four at a time, although most take greater care of them than Mr Al Fayed. These have included London goldsmith Gerald Benney, the General Trading Company in Chelsea, and the florist Edward Goodyear. Land Rover and Hatchards the Piccadilly booksellers also had the full set for a while, but after losing the patronage of the Queen Mother in a much publicised furore, the last of these relinquished the right to her Arms shortly afterwards.

As the Hatchards and Harrods examples indicate, the granting of a Warrant is very much the personal gift of the Royal in question. Because of this, the nature and business of the Warrant-holders, both past and present, provide an intriguing snapshot of life in the Palace as well as bearing witness to the enormous variety and diversity of goods enjoyed by the monarch and her family – and indeed by her predecessors.

The many and varied trades listed during the reign of George III, for example, include a Pin Maker (Tho. Trott) and a Mole-Taker (Fr. Dyer). Even the Rat Catcher gets a mention, although a discreet silence descends over the activities of one Andrew Cook of Holborn Hill, London. He publicly claimed to 'have cured 16,000 beds with great applause' and to have operated with great success within the precincts of the Royal Palace, but, unsurprisingly perhaps, no Warrant was ever granted to a Bug Exterminator. (That said, it is likely that anyone fulfilling such a role would have been one of the Palace's busiest functionaries in the pestilential London of the late eighteenth century.)

Much the same polite discretion is still encountered today, and a bar on the professions means that royal bankers, brokers, doctors and lawyers can neither be granted nor hold Warrants. Even so, more than two centuries on, curiosities can still be found in the lists. Among the more recent entries in the roll of royal tradesmen and women one finds a horse milliner and a pyrotechnician, as well as manufacturers of seaside rock, 'tubular equipment', paper plates and even lamprey pies. Less surprising, given what we know of royal preferences in this more open age, are the likes of Gibson Saddlers, which supplies colourful racing silks to Her Majesty, James Purdey & Sons and Holland & Holland (both gunsmiths to the Duke of Edinburgh, the one supplying shotguns, the other rifles), and Ainsworth's Pharmacy just off Harley Street, which has supplied homeopathic medicines to the Prince of Wales.

Lovers of tradition will note, too, that in spite of the aforementioned ten-year rule, many of the very earliest Warrants survived for generations. Garrard & Co. in Regent Street was Crown Jeweller to William IV and still holds a warrant from Prince Charles, and, as a young princess, Victoria drank soda water supplied by J. Schweppe and Company. Similarly, Mr James Swaine was Whip Maker to George III and, today, Swaine Adeney Brigg still supplies whips to the Royal Mews and umbrellas to Prince Charles. Other longstanding suppliers, including Twinings in the Strand, Crosse & Blackwell (late of Soho Square), locksmiths Chubb, and Gieves & Hawkes – the best-known name in Savile Row, if by no means the most exclusive – have all held their Warrants for well over one hundred years and thus through several reigns.

Significantly, and with only very few exceptions, the Warrants are granted to an individual within the company rather than to the company itself. Because of this, one sees that while the Victorian era was very much a man's world, proximity to Victoria herself lent an altogether different air to the proceedings. In fact, the first Empress of India saw fit to appoint no fewer than two dozen tradeswomen, mostly skilled artisans engaged in work of a feminine or at least delicate nature, such as Anne Maria Dillon, who made bookmarks; Emma Peachey, who created wax flowers;

and Mrs Anna Ede, who tailored the royal robes. (A century later, Ede and Ravenscroft is still thriving as a robe-maker, and has a trio of Royal Warrants to prove it.)

More unexpected perhaps was Mrs Marianna Dent, who made chronometers, and the mysterious mineralogist Mrs Mawe – but then suppliers have never been anything but varied. While often assumed to be for luxury goods only, Royal Warrants are regularly granted for supplies of the mundane and everyday, as well as the thoroughly up-to-date. Sony UK, to cite one famous name, has a warrant for supplying Prince Charles with state-of-the-art hi-fi equipment and, for many years, Edwards of Camberwell, located on a busy crossing in the dingy south-east London suburb, was the official provider of mopeds to Her Majesty. Other Royal Warrant holders supply carpets and carpet-cleaning products, dog food, drapery and lampshades.

Admittedly, it is still the more obviously prestigious products that attract the most attention and, even now, for every sauce manufacturer on the list (HP, Lea and Perrins) you'll find half a dozen purveyors of champagne. Similarly, every animal-feed supplier is balanced by a Berry Bros. or Fortnum's, and will always be the ones to benefit most from their status as suppliers to the Palace.

How else to explain why John Barbour & Sons, manufacturers of the almost ubiquitous dark-green 'Thornproof' jacket, so strongly values its brace of Warrants? It is the Royal Warrants that make perfumers Floris of Jermyn Street and Penhaligon in nearby Covent Garden smell so sweet, and that explain why, if Wilkinson Sword still has the edge over the upstart Gillette, it has more to do with ceremonial blades than disposable ones. When even a retailer as distinguished and exclusive as hatter James Lock – the oldest shop in London (see below) – displays its Warrants so prominently, you know that they believe that, after more than 800 years, royal connections still count.

LONDON'S OLDEST SHOPS

1676	Lock & Co.	Hatter	St James's Street
1689	Ede & Ravenscroft	Tailoring	Chancery Lane
1698	Berry Bros & Rudd	Wine	St James's Street
1706	Twinings & Co.	Tea	Strand
1707	Fortnum & Mason	Grocers	Piccadilly
1750	Swaine Adeney Brigg	Leather	Piccadilly Arcade
1760	Hamleys	Toys	Regent Street
1787	J. J. Fox	Cigars	St James's Street
1797	Hatchards	Bookseller	Piccadilly
*c.*1800	D. R. Harris	Chemist	St James's Street
1805	Truefitt & Hill	Barber	St James's Street
1830	James Smith	Umbrellas	New Oxford Street

Suits You, Sir

The decidedly masculine enclave centred on Savile Row has often been described as a club, but, in truth, the rag trade's most favoured address is more of a village – meaning it comes with everything that such a description implies.

For example, one's first impression of the place is that it has a definite air of self-containment, not to say a certain smugness. Peering out at you through their windows, the locals seem not to welcome visitors particularly – nor any sign of change – and like many small rural communities they clearly value their own way of doing things. Similarly, new arrivals are still regarded as outsiders, and will continue to be described in this way for at least the first three or four decades after their arrival.

The Row's residents are also not averse to squabbling among themselves, the usual argument being between tradition and change, although one suspects that even the oldest of the old guard privately acknowledge that change will win in the end. (In a street where family connections can survive seven or eight generations, that makes some of them very old indeed, but quite reasonably their concern is mostly to see that any attempts at progress are introduced with sufficient stealth that nobody, and certainly no customers, will realise that anything is changing.)

Most recently, the blue touchpaper was ignited by Messrs. Gieves & Hawkes, by far the best-known name in Savile Row, although by no means the oldest. (As separate entities they clothed both Wellington and Nelson, but the two names were joined together only as recently as the mid-1970s. Contrast that with H. Huntsman, which was already well-established the 1840s, and Henry Poole & Co., which arrived on the scene a good forty years before that.)

It was the company's decision to go headlong into ready-to-wear clothing that ignited the furore and, to make matters worse, the man striking the match was not just an outsider but someone from the very different world of fashion. He came by way of Calvin Klein and Reiss, but the decision was probably inevitable anyway if only because (as one rival put it) one can't build a business on old customers who are just about to die. But in a place that frowns on made-to-measure, never mind off-the-peg (as opposed to proper, 24-carat, copper-bottomed bespoke), it was bound to send shockwaves up the street. And it did, even before it emerged that the new collection was to include not just suits but foreign stuff, too – such as leather jackets and Italian-made jeans.

Of course, a measure of conservatism is only to be expected here, as indeed is a certain pride in the English way of doing things. The gentleman's suit originated in London, after all, as Samuel Pepys noted in his diary for 15 October 1666 after witnessing the arrival in Parliament of Charles II sporting a 'long cassock close to the body; of black cloth, and pinked in white silk under it, and a coat over it'. And even now Savile Row's global pre-eminence is such that the word for suit in Japanese is '*sebiro*', a straightforward transliteration.

That said, the experience of being fitted for a suit can be a little daunting – and not just because of the cost (which typically starts not that far south of £3,000). Everything about the place is designed to impress, and so it does, from your first sniff of its authentically old-fashioned ambience to the staff's amusingly dusty demeanour as they take you through the myriad choices from Huddersfield worsteds (or mohair worsteds for summer wear) through Scottish tweeds – Lowland, Harris and Shetland – to authentic West of England flannel.

Then there is the quietly assertive way – more dismissive than intentionally rude – in which a customer's physical peculiarities are noted as the measuring tape passes around his body: 'Dropped right shoulder . . . legs not quite even . . . is that how Sir *normally* stands?' And, of course, the chilling recognition that, as you walked through the door, the staff would unthinkingly have clocked and assessed what you equally unthinkingly decided to wear when getting dressed that morning.

It is at least reassuring to know that, as a customer, you are in good company, but also somewhat humbling in a place such as the aforementioned Henry Poole to know that where you are now, Queen Victoria and her family once went . . . as well as our own Queen, Tsar Alexander II, Churchill, Chaplin, and even the real Buffalo Bill. (Napoleon III and de Gaulle were regulars in Savile Row, too, which must say something for the reputation of French tailoring.)

Perhaps any uncomfortable sense of awe or unease could be minimised by reflecting on the fact that however lordly the practitioners of these arts appear, one is dealing with 'trade' – and pretty low trade at that. The splendid house of Huntsman, for example, was originally a gaiter and breeches maker. The august Mr Poole, 'founder of Savile Row', was in reality a humble draper who stumbled accidentally into tailoring after stitching his own military tunic. And even the great Henry Maxwell, the street's most famous bootmaker, started out fashioning spurs in a primitive forge in his own back yard.

But actually such snobbish assertions as these don't help at all. All these men were true craftsmen, and their descendants still are. They are the real deal, still the best in the world, and so in their own way every inch as aristocratic as any of their most distinguished customers.

Besides which, consider this: you don't make it in this business without exceptional skill and you don't survive for two centuries in any business – let alone one as mercurial and mendacious as this one – by being staid, stuffy, a stick-in-the-mud or anything less than really very, very good at what you do.

This, of course, is why a Savile Row suit can cost as much as a small car. And also why the people who produce them still strive, as they always have, to produce clothes that combine comfort with elegance, and quality with good taste, and that make a nod toward the fashion of the day while fully honouring what made sense in the past. In Savile Row, you don't just buy a suit, you don't just buy a piece of history. You buy something that will look better next year than this, better still the year after that, and that twenty years from now will be somewhat worn (in a good way) but still perfectly robust and absolutely serviceable.

10

Green London

'How sweet the morning air is!
See how that one little cloud floats like a pink feather
from some gigantic flamingo?
Now the red rim of the sun pushes itself over the
London cloud-bank.'

Sherlock Holmes in *The Sign of Four*
by Sir Arthur Conan Doyle

Shuffling toe-to-heel down Oxford Street, stuck solid in the rush-hour or choking on bus fumes at Farringdon, it's hard to believe that overcrowded London, its population now at a 100-year peak, is still one of the greenest and most open cities anywhere in the world. It's not just because of what Pitt the Elder called London's 'great lungs' – the more than 6,000 acres of Epping Forest on the one side (owned by the City of London Corporation), and on the other that great arc of historic parks and gardens at Bushy and Hampton Court, Syon, Osterley, Richmond and Kew. Nor, indeed, the well-known 'cultivated wildness' of Hampstead Heath or Hyde Park, the former another possession of the City's and the latter a somewhat surprising survivor, including as it does 350 acres of some of the most valuable land anywhere on earth.

In fact, what makes London so green are the many lesser-known parks and gardens, many hundreds of them, from the deceptively lush shrubberies in the likes of Bedford, Russell and St James's squares, through the tree-lined walks of Battersea Park and the Thames embankments to those hidden enclaves that make up the lawyers' ancient Inns of Court and – by far the best of all – the more than forty high-walled acres complete with a vast lake, flamingoes, rare shrubs and who knows what other delights Her Majesty gets to enjoy.

Admittedly, an invitation to the regular summer garden parties affords a few of us a brief glimpse of what lies behind the Palace walls, but there are, even so, many other open spaces that offer easier access for anyone in search of what in London at least passes for peace and tranquillity. Of these, some are astonishingly large, but others so small you wonder how they came to be and how they have survived. In their own ways, all offer visitors the chance to make a brief escape from the streets, to get away from the hurly-burly and the sheer breathless pace of contemporary city life.

Peaceful Postman's Park, for example, so called because of its proximity once to the old GPO building behind St Paul's, could not provide a greater contrast to the hard-faced, high-rise office blocks that are its neighbours. Popular with city workers who come to kick off their shoes at lunchtime, to snatch a quick cigarette or sneak a bit of sunshine, it is also where the celebrated Victorian painter G. F. Watts proposed siting a national memorial to the heroism of ordinary people.

Here, on a long wall beneath a wooden awning, ceramic plaques celebrate the selfless heroism of fifty-three ordinary men, women and, especially, children. The otherwise unsung heroes include: Alice Ayres, a labourer's daughter 'who by intrepid conduct saved three children from a burning house at the cost of her own young life'; Thomas Simpson, who 'died of exhaustion after saving many lives from the breaking ice at Highgate Ponds'; and brave little Harry Sisley of Kilburn, who was just ten years old in 1878 when he drowned attempting to rescue his baby brother.

ZSL – NOAH'S PARK

As described elsewhere in this chapter, James I introduced pet crocodiles, camels and even an elephant to St James's Park, but historically most royal animals were kept in the royal menagerie at the Tower of London and continued to be so for more than 600 years. In medieval times, these included three leopards, a lion and – from 1252 – Britain's first ever polar bear, a gift to Henry III from King Haakon IV of Norway. Three years later, the bear was joined by an African elephant, which arrived by boat as a gift from France's Louis IX, and later still by another lion, a tiger, a lynx, a wolf, a porcupine and an eagle.

In the sixteenth century, it was felt necessary to erect a special viewing platform for privileged visitors 'to stande on to see the Lyons lett out' – and by the time they began to admit the public it was becoming clear that the Tower of London was no longer the ideal place to house a collection of such large and rare beasts.

Around London at the time, there had long been a number of private collections, such as the one run by a family of circus owners on the Strand. From 1733, they started displaying cages of lions, tigers, monkeys and other exotic species, among the most celebrated of which was an elephant called Chunee. He once stole Lord Byron's hat, and appeared in panto at Drury Lane, but was eventually driven mad by his years in captivity. So much so, indeed, that the beast unfortunately killed his keeper and then went on the rampage. As bystanders fled, musket-wielding soldiers were called in to silence the animal, two of them discharging a remarkable 152 rounds before the *coup de grace* was delivered with a dagger. Sadly, even then the elephant's torments weren't over, with Londoners queuing to pay a shilling to see his carcass being butchered and his skeleton going on display in Piccadilly. Eventually removed to the Royal College of Surgeons, the bullet holes still clearly visible, Chunee's bones were finally destroyed in an air raid in 1941.

All too often, the animals in the royal menagerie fared little better. A pair of ostriches, for example, had died after being fed more than eighty nails by keepers labouring under the misapprehension – common at the time – that the flightless giants could digest iron. (The elephant belonging to James I had similarly been fed a daily ration of red wine, in the belief that during the summer months at least elephants were unable to drink water.) Then there was the ape that was beaten to death after hurling a 9 lb cannonball at an onlooker.

In 1831, it was finally decided that enough was enough, and a decision was taken by William IV to donate the animals to the Zoological Society of London. Recently established by Royal Charter in Regent's Park, the first of its kind anywhere in the world, it would provide the animals with practical enclosures, appropriate food and staff who knew what they were doing. The 'zoo' as it became known – the first time the word was coined – would also give scientists an opportunity to observe the animals at close quarters, and the public a chance to engage with species hitherto only glimpsed in storybooks.

Inevitably, some inhabitants had broader appeal than others and, over the years, several of the zoo's residents have achieved near-celebrity status.

1850 – Obaysch the Hippopotamus

The arrival of Europe's first hippo since Roman times caused such excitement in London that visitor numbers to the zoo actually doubled. Almost as popular was the Quagga, which famously became the only live example of this subspecies of South African zebra to be photographed because, by 1870, the remainder had been hunted to extinction. (More recently the Quagga also became the first extinct species to have its DNA studied.)

1865 – Jumbo the Elephant

Travelling with P. T. Barnum's famous circus, history's most famous elephant tragically died after being hit by a train in Canada in 1885. Before joining the circus, however, he lived in Regent's Park, his immense size giving a new word to the English language. Loud protests greeted the decision to sell the beast to Barnum for $10,000 (about £150,000 in today's terms) – 10,000 children wrote to Queen Victoria to try to reverse the decision – but the sale went ahead.

1914 – Winnie the Bear

At the start of the Great War, a junior army officer posted to Europe with troops from Canada presented the zoo with a North American black bear. Lt Harry Colebourn had named the bear after his home town of Winnipeg and, like many children, Christopher Robin Milne named his teddy bear after the animal following a visit to Regent's

Park with his writer-father, Alan Alexander Milne. The rest, as they say, is history.

1947 – Guy the Gorilla

When another European war threatened, the animals were removed to the relative safety of Whipsnade in Bedfordshire. (Only one died as result of enemy action – a young giraffe, which succumbed to shock after a bomb exploded nearby.) When the zoo reopened, a new arrival (on Guy Fawkes Day 1947) was a baby gorilla, immediately winning the hearts of the public when he was photographed clutching a hot-water bottle against the November chill. Guy was the original gentle giant – he frequently caught sparrows in his giant paws before letting them fly off – sadly dying at the age of 32 during a dental operation.

1949 – Brumas the Polar Bear

The first polar bear bred in Britain, Brumas – named after keepers Bruce and Sam – was so popular that, in 1950, visitor numbers peaked at three million, a figure that has still not been surpassed. Brumas was actually female, but an early press article reported otherwise and, in the public's mind, the mistake was never put right.

1950 – Eros the Snowy Owl

Seeking shelter from a storm on board the Royal Navy's HMS *Eros*, this splendid bird lived at the zoo for more than forty years during which time he fathered nearly sixty chicks. (Other particularly long-lived residents have included Belinda the Mexican red-kneed spider and another polar bear, Pipaluk, both of whom survived into their early twenties.)

1965 – Goldie the Golden Eagle

Zoo animals occasionally make a break for it and, in the mid-1960s, central London literally ground to a halt when thousands of motorists stopped in the park so they could watch Goldie swooping from tree to tree. Successfully evading capture – and gaining a mention during Prime Minister's Questions – Goldie was eventually returned to his enclosure after spending a couple of hours short of twelve days on the wing.

At Lincoln's Inn Fields, a dozen acres of lawns and plane trees overlooked by the collegiate buildings of the lawyers are surprisingly quiet, too (given the proximity of noisy High Holborn). So quiet, indeed, that it is hard to believe that this is where, in the late sixteenth century, many thousands of Protestant revellers gathered to witness the grisly execution of fourteen Catholic traitors. Sentenced to be hanged, drawn and quartered for a plot to oust Good Queen Bess in favour of her cousin Mary, the leader, Sir Anthony Babington, was reportedly still fully conscious when his evisceration began.

Equally hard to credit is that (as previously noted, in the 1930s) the authorities ordered these lovely gardens to be dug up, excavating many hundreds of yards of deep trenches and armoured bunkers. In the event, they were never used, and who knows what purpose, if any, they serve now?

No less strange is Coram's Fields in nearby Bloomsbury, if only because its pleasures are strictly off-limits to adults unless they are accompanied by a child. Occupying the site of a wealthy seafarer's Foundling Hospital, a niche in a pillar by the roadside once housed a revolving 'All-Comers Basket' into which unmarried mothers could deposit their unwanted infants.

On the first day, more than one hundred were left in this manner, and with more than four times that number arriving in the days that followed, hospital staff were quickly swamped. It was obvious that this well-meaning but random and chaotic admissions policy had to be abandoned, and eventually the hospital went too, although fortunately a new one was created around the corner in Great Ormond Street. The site was developed but, happily, nine acres of gardens were saved by the newspaper proprietor Viscount Rothermere, thereby giving children kind enough to treat their parents to a day out somewhere green and pleasant to go and play.

Fortunately, adults are free to wander through the Royal Parks unaccompanied, but it wasn't always so. For years, many hundreds of acres of wilderness were set aside for hunting deer with the public rarely being granted access, and when they were, they were given strict instructions to behave. Queen Anne, for example, largely restricted access to 'foreign ministers, nobility, Parliament and the Queen's household'. King James I similarly had a large menagerie in St James's Park (see panel above), but very much for his own pleasure rather than the public's. Later, there were aviaries here, too, along the side of what is now Birdcage Walk. And George II's wife made a concerted effort to claim both St James's Park and Hyde Park for herself, despite the public having, by this time, enjoyed reasonably good access to both since the 1670s.

Happily, Queen Caroline failed in her bid – although nearly 300 acres of Hyde Park were pinched to create Kensington Gardens – but there are still plenty of reminders of the days when the parks were the sovereign's personal domain. There are, for example, some pretty odd regulations, such as it being illegal for anyone in a bath chair to travel three abreast through Hyde Park. And while it is true that no one any longer needs a key to enter any of the Royal Parks, we are nevertheless still forbidden to brandish a sword in such a place or touch a pelican without written permission. (Pelicans are a bit of a tradition here, incidentally: in 1664, the Russian ambassador presented a pair of birds to Charles II and, nearly 350 years later, they are still a popular gift from foreign ambassadors newly appointed to the Court of St James's.)

In Hyde Park, one can at least now ride a horse along Rotten Row, but once upon a time this, too, was a royal prerogative. The name indeed is a corruption of the French '*route de roi*' or 'king's road', dating from the end of the seventeenth century when William III, an asthmatic, moved the court out of town to Kensington Palace. Finding the walk to St James's too dangerous, he installed some 300 oil lamps along his new road, making it the first artificially lit highway in the country.

St James's Park is far smaller than Hyde Park but nevertheless perhaps the best of them, with its famous waterfowl – every native species of duck, apparently, and then some – which are lucky enough to have their own private Duck Island to escape to when the crowds of visitors become too much.

The ornamental Swiss cottage on the island is a nice example of nineteenth-century kitsch and was built by the Ornithological Society of London. With typical Victorian ingenuity, its designer included an elaborate steam-heating mechanism for the efficient incubation of eggs. And while the modern concrete footbridge may be no match for the 1857 original – an elegant suspension design – looking west from it the view across the lake still offers walkers one of the best prospects the whole of London has to offer.

In particular, the exotic silhouettes of Horse Guards and Whitehall Court, with their spikey towers and domes, contrasts wonderfully with the big wheel of the London Eye and provides a perfect counterpoint to the magical reflections of the park's gnarled old trees.

When it comes to old trees, however, Regent's Park claims the prize thanks to a clutch of fossilised stumps situated by its own lake in the Inner Circle. The last surviving remnant of the defunct Victorian-era Royal Botanic Society, these are perfectly genuine and quite an extraordinary thing to stumble upon in the middle of a twenty-first-century city.

And speaking of stumbling, next time you're in St James's Square take a closer look at the statue of King William III in the centre. See that small hump under the horse's left rear leg? That represents the molehill upon which His Majesty's mount stumbled in 1702, throwing the king to a prolonged and ignoble death. The anniversary of this unhappy event was marked for many years by Bonnie Prince Charlie's men, who – traitors to a man – used to drink a grateful toast to 'the little gentleman in black velvet'.

Of course, other parks have their peculiarities too: the gardeners in Soho Square, for example, keep their tools in a rustic, octagonal, Tudor-style summerhouse, while those in Grosvenor Gardens store theirs in a pair of tiny, folly pavilions decorated with literally thousands of seashells. The pair was a gift from a grateful French nation after the Second World War and, in return, we put up a large equestrian statue of their Marshal Ferdinand Foch.

Perhaps the most curious building, however, is the large Art Nouveau rotunda in King Edward Memorial Park in Shadwell on the north bank of the Thames. No mere folly, despite its fancy brickwork and elaborate appearance, this not-so-mini-colosseum is actually an over-decorated flue designed to vent noxious fumes from Rotherhithe Tunnel. These days, cars and trucks are to blame but somewhat less than 100 years ago the culprits would have had legs rather than wheels. The tunnel originally provided a route for horse-drawn wagons to reach the docks, something that explains the narrowness of the carriageways and the severity of the bends, which continue to cause problems for larger vehicles attempting to cross from north to south.

WHATEVER THE WEATHER

Something of a hotspot in the capital, Camden Square, NW1, has twice achieved record-breaking monthly temperatures: 29.4 °C in May 1949 and 35.6 °C in June 1957.

By contrast, in January 1963, Kew Gardens experienced a period of nine days on the trot when the daytime temperature didn't rise above 0 °C. The same week, Arsenal FC had to cancel a fixture with the pitch under 8 in. of snow.

In November 1665, a deep depression was recorded over London, thought to be the lowest ever, of 931 millibars, while December 1796 saw the capital's coldest single day when the temperature plunged to -21.1 °C at Greenwich. A few days later, it was still only -19 °C.

Overall, London's coldest ever year was almost certainly 1684, when the Thames froze in central London from bank to bank, to a depth of 11 in., and remained that way for nearly two months. (Albeit for shorter periods this happened a further fifteen times, the last being in 1814, which was the year of the final 'Frost Fair'.)

Improved water flow through better bridges means such ice-ups no longer occur in central London, but they still happen further upstream. In 1963 at Kingston-upon-Thames, it was briefly possible to walk from one bank to the other.

In January 1928, a storm surge in the North Sea travelled up the Thames, killing fourteen and flooding the homes of around 4,000 Londoners as well as many public buildings.

In 1873, London notched up a record-breaking run of seventy-four foggy days. Since then, the worst pea-souper was in December 1952, which led to as many as 12,000 deaths – from respiratory illness as well as accidents involving people who couldn't see traffic – and some 100,000 cases of medical illness.

On 14 August 1975, nearly 7 in. of rain fell on Hampstead in just over two hours, flooding many houses. Two people were struck by lightning, one man drowned, and then huge hailstones fell on the same area, creating what one meteorologist described as 'a sea of icy porridge'.

In January 1977, a single piece of ice weighing 110 lb – something called a hydrometeor – smashed into a house in Ponder's End. A few years earlier, two more had wrecked homes in Isleworth and Fulham.

On 2 June 1975, the *Guardian* reported that snow had fallen on Lord's Cricket Ground, interrupting a game between Middlesex and Surrey. One reader insisted this was untrue, as previously London's latest snowfall had been in May 1821. He complained to the Press Council but the enquiry found in the journalist's favour – snow had indeed fallen in June.

11

Eccentrics' London

'I think London is sexy because it's so full of eccentrics.'

Rachel Weisz

2nd Duke of Buckingham (1628–87)

Fortunate enough to inherit several priceless acres between the river and the Strand, George Villiers' London estate included fifty houses, ten cottages, four stable blocks and seven interconnecting gardens – and a sumptuous ducal palace before his debts got out of hand and he lost the lot to developers.

Somewhat eccentrically, he insisted that in return the new owners commemorate his period as landowner, and to do this by using every element of his name when naming the new streets they were building. The developers obliged, creating Buckingham Street, Villiers Street, Duke Street, George Street and even Of Alley – although the latter was subsequently renamed York Place by po-faced councillors.

Hon. Charles Hamilton (1704–86)

The 9th of the Earl of Abercorn's fourteen children designed much of Holland Park for Lord Holland and, on his own behalf, spent almost every pound he had building England's first landscaped park. Situated close to where the modern A3 crosses the M25, items of expenditure on his estate at Painshill included £700 (at 1738 prices) for anyone prepared to dress like a hermit and live alone in a cave for a year.

No one took him up on his offer, but the rest of the cash went on moving hills, excavating valleys and building more than a dozen follies around an expensively dug twenty-acre lake. Hamilton spent so much, in fact, there was nothing left to pay for a house and, after selling the land at a huge loss, Hamilton retired to Bath and shortly afterwards died.

Hon. Henry Cavendish (1731–1810)

An early prototype of a barking-mad boffin, Cavendish remains all but unknown despite discovering the chemical compositions of water and air. When attending scientific meetings, he preferred not to speak to anyone and, at home in Clapham, had letterboxes installed in all the internal doors so that servants could write to him rather than conversing with him directly.

Instead of friends, he filled this and another vast house in Bedford Square with scientific equipment and books, spending many millions on their acquisition while acting as his own librarian to save the cost of engaging a professional. After his death, he was found to own more bank stock than anyone else in England, but never spent more than five shillings on a meal.

Martin van Butchell (1735–1814)

When Mrs van B died in 1775, this successful dentist had her eyes replaced with marbles, her body embalmed with camphor and turpentine and the whole ensemble painted to appear more lifelike, before being put on display in the window of his Mount Street, Mayfair, surgery. In the face of protests from neighbours, he insisted his marriage contract allowed such a thing, perhaps because he could draw an income from his wife's estate as long as she remained at home and above ground.

Unsurprisingly, both the protests and the queues of gawpers grew as the body began to decompose, but not until van Butchell's death in 1814 was the spectacle finally dealt with. In 1815, his son presented the mouldering corpse to the Royal College of Surgeons and, in 1944, what remained of Mrs van Butchell was blown to bits by a German bomb.

8th Earl of Bridgewater (1756–1829)

Inheriting £40,000 a year but worth barely ten when he died, Francis Henry Egerton was a major benefactor of the British Museum but preferred Paris to London and settled there despite knowing more Latin than French. To Parisians, he became the archetype of an eccentric English 'milord', travelling everywhere with sixteen carriages and a retinue of thirty servants, and equipping his pets with silver collars and expensively hand-tooled doggy boots and doggy coats.

For sport, Bridgewater filled his tiny city garden with hundreds of rabbits, pigeons and partridges, taking pot shots at them when he was in the mood. When he died, he left each of his servants a cocked hat and three pairs of stockings, insisting they keep the house running for a further two months as if he were still alive, which they duly did.

10th Duke of Hamilton & Brandon (1767–1852)

A man who collected titles as others collect stamps, London-born Alexander Hamilton inherited two dukedoms, a brace of marquessates, four earldoms and seven baronies. He was known as '*magnifico*', but only sarcastically once his sense of self-worth had led him to declare that he was the rightful King of Scotland.

Convinced that he would be called to witness the Second Coming, he spent £130,000 on a vast mausoleum – millions in today's terms – and another £11,000 on an Egyptian sarcophagus for himself. Unfortunately, this was so small that his feet had to be cut off in order to squeeze him in.

5th Duke of Portland (1800–79)

The intensely reclusive owner of 110 acres of the West End, at his house in Cavendish Square William John Cavendish Cavendish-Scott-Bentinck erected an 80-ft-high screen of frosted glass around the garden so no one could watch him arriving or see him wandering around.

On his Nottinghamshire estate, His Grace went further still, employing 15,000 workmen to dig tunnels beneath his stately home as well as an underground riding school – he never rode – and three underground ballrooms in which no one danced. Preferring to eat nothing but roast chicken, the Duke remained unmarried.

Sir Edward Watkin (1819–1901)

Honouring a longstanding English tradition of animosity towards the French, having failed in his bid to build the first Channel Tunnel, in 1891 the Metropolitan Railway magnate set out to out-Eiffel the Eiffel Tower by building something similar but bigger on a grassy hill in Wembley. Public enthusiasm was enormous – 100,000 turned up to see the work begin – but it quickly died away together with the money.

Designed to soar 1,175 ft into the sky, ground subsidence, poor foundations and Watkin's increasingly poor health meant it struggled to reach a tenth of that. When work on it stopped, it turned out to be worth less as scrap than it would cost to demolish, and for a few years it stood like an embarrassing rusty monument to Victorian bombast.

Eventually, in 1907, a decision was taken to blow it up, and in 1923 the site was cleared to make way for Wembley Stadium.

Sir Francis Galton (1822–1911)

A cousin of Charles Darwin's, Galton was a genuine polymath who pioneered the use of fingerprinting, devised numerous powerful statistical methods, drew the world's first ever weather map, paved the way for what we now call differential psychology, and established and funded a new professorial chair at London University.

Unfortunately for Galton's reputation, the chair was in Eugenics, a system he devised of racial theories that were subsequently adopted by the Nazis and so are now rightly discredited. He also spent years mapping Britain to establish where the most beautiful women lived (London, he decided), and insisted on wearing what he termed 'Galton's Universal Patent Ventilating Hat' in the sincere belief that if his head overheated he would fall in a fit to the floor.

Francis Buckland (1826–80)

Confronting a problem well understood today – too many mouths, not enough food – Francis Buckland founded the Society for the Acclimatisation of Animals in a bid to persuade Londoners to adopt a more varied diet. Its inaugural dinner was held in King Street, St James's, in 1862, with a menu that included elephant trunk soup, sliced porpoise head and rhino pie.

Interestingly, horse was not on the menu. With hippophilia so embedded among the aristocracy, Buckland firmly believed that 'hippophagy has not the slightest chance of success in this country'. London Zoo provided plenty of alternatives, however, including some panther chops to go with Buckland's ants and earwigs, Japanese sea-slugs, kangaroo, parrot and wild boar. The experiment failed, of course, but probably only because Buckland was somewhat ahead of his time.

Julius Drewe (1856–1931)

The founder of London's Home & Colonial Stores built a colossal fortune from retail but then sold up and settled down to spend it. Convinced by an unscrupulous genealogist that he was descended from one of the Conqueror's lieutenants, Drewe set out to honour his ancestor Drogo de Teign by building a vast, medieval-style castle down in Devon.

Designed by Sir Edwin Lutyens, Castle Drogo unfortunately took so long to build that, by the time Drewe moved on to the 1,500-acre estate, he had only two months left to live. The last castle ever to be built in Britain soon afterwards became the first twentieth-century property to be acquired by the National Trust, which still owns it today.

5th Earl of Lonsdale (1857–1944)

As befitting a president of the Automobile Association, Henry Cecil Lowther conceived the strongest possible liking for its bright yellow livery. Back home in Leicestershire, he ordered new yellow uniforms for the servants, yellow cardigans for his outdoor staff and demanded that all estate vehicles – even down to the wheelbarrows – be repainted the same hue.

Also a founding member of the National Sporting Club in Covent Garden, in 1908 he bet the American banker J. P. Morgan an incredible £21,000 (nearly £2 million today) that a man could walk solo round the world while finding a wife and supporting himself by selling postcards. He later conceived the famous boxing belts that still bear his name, coughing up the cash for their 22 ct gold decoration.

Sir George Reresby Sitwell (1860–1943)

Banning electricity from his household, attempting to barter for his son's Eton education with pigs and potatoes, and having Chinese willow patterns stencilled on a herd of cows, when the London-born baronet failed to persuade Selfridges to stock his Sitwell Egg (a 'portable meal' of rice, smoked meat and artificial lime) he retired to his Derbyshire estate and applied himself to feverish inventing.

For this, he set aside seven individual studies, and over time produced such must-have devices as a musical toothbrush and a miniature revolver for dispatching wasps. Unfortunately, his attempts at making knife-handles from condensed milk met with little success, and the government of the day remained unpersuaded by his plan to manufacture military gas masks using discarded peach stones.

12th Duke of St Albans (1875–1964)

Osborne de Vere Beauclerk, 12th Duke of St Albans, Earl of Burford, Baron Vere of Hanworth and of Heddington – but more informally known as 'Obby' – was a direct descendant of Nell Gwynn and, as one of Charles II's numerous illegitimate offspring, held the office of Hereditary Grand Falconer of England.

By 1953, the title had long been irrelevant, but Obby was determined to make it work for him and planned to exercise his right to take a live bird to the Coronation. On being told by Westminster Abbey officials that only a stuffed one would be acceptable, he declined to join his fellow dukes in the pews and stayed at home. His Grace later left for America, where he travelled coast to coast by Greyhound bus and claimed to have received sixty-eight proposals of marriage.

14th Baron Berners (1883–1950)

Setting out from 40 Half Moon Street in a Rolls-Royce fitted with a piano in the back, the composer and diplomat Lord Berners doubtless raised the odd eyebrow. At home on his Oxfordshire estate at Farringdon, he could really let fly though, his bachelor lifestyle leaving him free to indulge himself however he saw fit.

In practice, this meant fitting his whippets with diamond-studded collars, dying pet doves to match his mood and, where possible, eating colour-coded meals in which each ingredient was chosen to be the same colour as the next. By far the *pièce de résistance*, however, was an elegant 140-ft folly in the grounds with a sign at the top warning 'Members of the Public Committing Suicide from this Tower Do So at their Own Risk'.

7th Duke of Leinster (1892–1976)

Edward Fitzgerald is almost certainly the only duke to lose a fortune without even laying his hands on the money. After running up huge debts in his youth, he sought to clear them by foolishly selling an inheritance worth millions for £60,000 and an allowance of just £1,000 a year.

Unfortunately he came into the dukedom early, and lived a very long time, so the money was never going to be enough for him. It soon ran out, and the man the papers had cruelly nicknamed the 'Bedsit Duke' was found dead in a single rented room in Pimlico.

Geoffrey Nathaniel Pyke (1893–1948)

Believing stockbrokers were as stupid as they looked (and proving it by making a killing in the City), Pyke dreamed of creating giant warships and aircraft carriers made of ice mixed with sawdust. After convincing Lord Mountbatten that such a vessel would be both torpedo-proof and unsinkable, he became one of Winston Churchill's favourite wartime boffins.

The ice mixture he called 'Pykrete' and – incredibly – it worked. Unfortunately, by the time the prototype was built and tested on a top-secret lake in Canada, the war was nearly over and the technology considered surplus to requirements. Pyke must have known he had missed his moment and, retreating to a bedsit in Hampstead, he subsequently took his own life.

Woodrow Wyatt (1918–97)

A former Labour MP who subsequently became one of Mrs Thatcher's most ardent admirers, Wyatt was rarely happier than when extolling the virtues of being an Englishman – as opposed to 'a chimpanzee or a flea, or a Frenchman or a German'. After setting out from his St John's Wood home for a tour of Europe, the prolific Fleet Street hack was asked by one French hotelier to spell his name, to which he replied, 'W-Y-A-T-T – as in Waterloo . . . Ypres . . . Agincourt . . . Trafalgar . . . Trafalgar.'

Joe Orton (1933–67)

With time on his hands before his career as a playwright really took off, Orton and boyfriend Kenneth Halliwell spent many hours defacing hundreds of library books by inserting inappropriate illustrations and typing a series of grotesque and often highly offensive reviews on the insides of their dust jackets.

Both were eventually jailed for six months for a total of 1,769 offences – and additionally fined 18*s.* 4*d.* for returning some of the books late. Soon after Orton's release, he found himself lionised by London's literary and dramatic élites and, fearing he was being edged out of his lover's new life, Halliwell murdered him at their Islington flat before killing himself.

Jungleyes Love (1956–2012)

While at Harrow School, Love (real name: Charles Gibaut Bissell-Thomas) wrote to the Chinese Embassy requesting 725 free copies of Mao's *Red Book*. These were duly delivered to the school and, just as quickly, returned by the masters, after which Love was suspended for writing to the headmaster of Latymer Upper School in West London asking for a place there instead.

He got the place, switched schools and – deciding never to cut or comb his hair again – grew such a long, matted mess of a mane that he could sit on it quite comfortably.

After taking a degree in neurobiology, he travelled to Asia, becoming a habitual user of hallucinogenic fly agaric and a lifelong fruitarian. Sadly, a lack of vitamin B in this diet combined with a bout of TB to finish him off in his fifties, but not before Love had become a familiar figure around Kew where he had a shop selling runic jewellery, dinosaur eggs and fossilised animal poo.

12

Eating London

'I think what's going on with gorillas is pretty bad. The fact is that you can buy gorilla meat in London any day you want it.'

Adam Ant

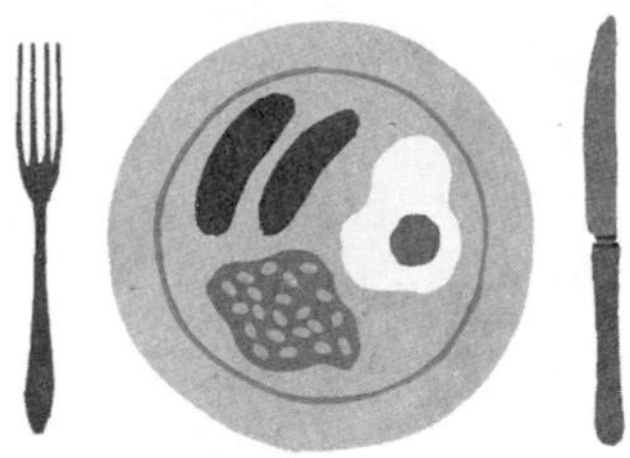

Dishes Invented in London

Scotch Eggs

The word 'tartan' is English and comes from the French '*tiretain*'; kilts were originally Norse, not Gaelic, and Anatolian Hittites were playing tunes on bagpipes as long ago as 1000 BC. Perhaps it's no surprise then that the Scotch egg isn't Scottish either. The first was invented in 1738 by staff at Fortnum and Mason in Piccadilly, and inspired by a traditional Mughal dish of boiled eggs stuffed inside a shell of ground lamb mixed with several spices called '*nargisi kofta*'. (The store was also the first to sell baked beans, incidentally, having bought H. J. Heinz's entire stock in 1866.)

Tinned Food

The means of preserving food in this way dates back to 1810 when a Hoxton merchant called Peter Durand patented a sealed metal canister after demonstrating that food could be safely sealed inside it for long periods. Unfortunately, his canisters had to be opened using a hammer – the invention of the can-opener was still more than fifty years away – and, in 1812, Durand sold his rights in the invention for £1,000.

Omelette Arnold Bennett

The popular early twentieth-century writer was a frequent guest at the Savoy, and on his behalf the kitchens created a rich egg dish of Parmesan cheese, smoked haddock and cream. While the name of the chef responsible has been lost – the celebrated Escoffier had been dismissed back in 1898, accused of conspiring with César Ritz to steal thousands of pounds' worth of wine – the omelette has remained on the menu ever since.

Chicken Tikka Masala

A perennially popular takeaway dish but one that, in the words of the *Daily Telegraph*, 'does not exist in Indian cuisine'. Chicken tikka masala is thought now to account for around 15 per cent of all the curries consumed in Britain, and while its inventor cannot be positively identified, the food writer Charles Campion has traced its origins to London in the 1970s. It was, he says, created 'so that the ignorant could have gravy with their chicken tikka'.

Wedding Cake

The tradition of having a tiered cake to celebrate a couple's nuptials is thought to have been inspired by the distinctive, stepped spire of St Bride's, Fleet Street. At 226 ft, it is the second-tallest Wren church in London – only St Paul's reaches higher.

It is a coincidence that female participants are known as 'brides', which is a word with German origins and nothing whatsoever to do with the diminutive of the Irish St Bridget.

Fish and Chips

Various rival claims have been made about who invented this most traditional of English meals but, in 1968, the National Federation of Fish Friers recognised that of Joseph Malin. Living in Cleveland Way, Whitechapel, in 1860, the Jewish émigré was the first to combine the staple of fried fish – brought into this country by Jewish refugees from seventeenth-century Spain and Portugal – with the newly fashionable chipped potato.

Twiglets

By 1929, Peek, Frean and Co. of Clements Road, Bermondsey, was one of the country's most successful biscuit-makers. Keen to expand after more than seventy years in the business, the company charged its French technical manager, Rondalin Zwadoodie, with the responsibility of coming up with an entirely new line. Zwadoodie experimented with the firm's Vitawheat dough and some yeast extract and, by Christmas that year, the savoury snack was perfected and on sale.

EXTRAORDINARY PLACES TO EAT

1820

When a new cross and ball were installed above the dome of St Paul's, the architect C. R. Cockerell celebrated by hosting a small luncheon inside the ball.

1827

Hoping to prove his new Thames Tunnel was safe, Marc Brunel held a banquet for forty VIPs beneath the Thames with music provided by the Coldstream Guards. It wasn't, however, and the tunnel flooded shortly afterwards.

1843

Before Nelson was finally hoisted into place, fourteen stonemasons sat down to a draughty, vertigo-inducing supper on top of the world's tallest Corinthian column.

1853

The pioneering palaeontologist who first coined the term 'dinosaur', Professor Richard Owen was among the guests at a New Year's Eve dinner held inside a life-size cement model of an iguanadon, which now stands in Crystal Palace Park.

1912

The sculpture of four horses and a chariot on top of the Wellington Arch at Hyde Park Corner is the work of Adrian Jones. On completing the monumental bronze – called *Quadriga* – he entertained seven guests to dinner inside it.

2009

Rootmaster, a so-called 'bustaurant', was a Brick Lane-based vegan eatery. It was housed on the top deck of a traditional red London bus, but has sadly closed.

2010

Located on Clerkenwell Green, the aptly named Dans le Noir invites diners to eat in pitch blackness, the room sealed off from all sources of light in order that the taste and texture of the food can be appreciated to the full.

Eating by Numbers

Each year at Wimbledon's All England Tennis Club, spectators, players and officials consume more than 60,000 lb of strawberries over the course of a fortnight, together with 1,850 gallons of cream and 17,000 bottles of Champagne.

At a typical Buckingham Palace garden party, 400 staff are involved in serving approximately 27,000 cups of tea, 20,000 sandwiches and 20,000 slices of cake.

The capital's largest-ever sporting event, the XXX Olympiad – a.k.a. London 2012 – posed even greater challenges and, during the course of the Games, deliveries to the athletes' village included 25,000 loaves of bread, 232 tons of potatoes and 82 tons of seafood, more than 100 tons of meat, 19 tons of eggs and 21 tons of cheese. Fruit and veg accounted for another 360 tons of deliveries.

Wembley Stadium has a total of 34 bars, 8 restaurants, 98 different kitchens and 688 food and drink service points. On match days, approximately 40,000 pints of beer can be served at half-time, while soft drinks can be dispensed by machine at a rate of nearly 3,000 a minute.

London's most expensive takeaway meal is thought to be an order of sushi from Ubon in Canary Wharf that was chauffeur-driven to Luton airport and flown out to the Azerbaijani capital Baku on one of Roman Abramovich's private jets. The cost of this has been estimated at £40,000.

In 1925, the world's largest banquet was held at Olympia in west London. According to a Pathé newsreel at the time, some 1,300 waitresses served 8,000 Freemasons seated at more than five miles of trestle tables arranged around the main exhibition hall.

Mayfair's Le Gavroche found its way into the *Guinness Book of World Records* in 1997 when three guests racked up a bill of £13,000. This dwarfed the experience of the diner who did a runner from the Connaught when his bill came to £986, but is in turn modest by the standards of One for One Park Lane where a single bottle of Armand de Brignac Champagne – admittedly quite a large one – could set you back £80,000.

13

Working London

'I would rather start out somewhere small, like London or England.'

Britney Spears

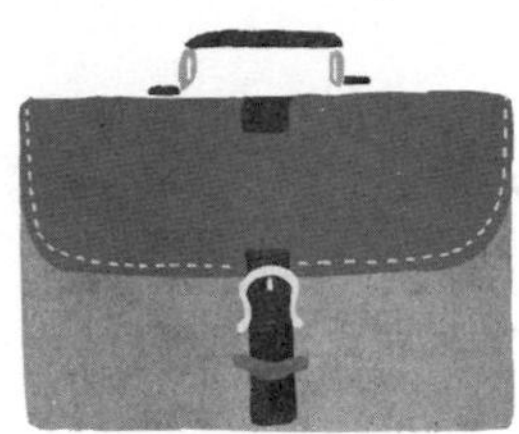

Odd Jobs – Something in the City

Traditionally a retired Army officer of senior rank, the **Constable of the Tower of London** – of which, in the course of nearly 1,000 years, there have been 159 – lives on site, has custody of the Crown Jewels and can still claim a number of extraordinary perks as part of the job. These include any horses, cattle, pigs or sheep that fall off London Bridge; the cargo of any wagons that fall into the moat; 6*s*. 8*d*. (just over 33p) from any vessel fishing between the Tower and Thames Estuary; and a shilling (5p) from those bringing herring into the City. He is also provided with a barrel of rum from any ship of the Royal Navy that ties up at Tower Wharf.

Still at the Tower, the **Yeoman Warder Ravenmaster** is responsible for the welfare of its iconic feathered guardians, each of which enjoys a daily ration of 6oz of raw meat from Smithfield and bird biscuits soaked in blood. There are seven birds in all – the six ordained by Charles II, plus a spare – and only one has ever been dismissed, for chewing television aerials. Such is their status that when a seventeenth-century Astronomer Royal complained that the birds were interfering with his observatory, he was packed off to Greenwich and the birds allowed to remain.

The post of **Royal Herb Strewer** dates back to the Stuart court, when the need was felt to shield the sovereign and his retinue from the filth and odour of the streets by strewing his path with aromatic herbs. For this, James II paid a woman £12 anually as 'garnisher and trimmer of the chapel, presence and privy lodgings', and today the role is still performed on ceremonial occasions by a female descendant of Anne Fellowes who filled the role at the Coronation of George IV.

The **Swanmarker**, an officer of the Royal Household, assists with the annual swan-upping ceremony, effectively a census of swans on certain reaches of the Thames. The sovereign owns all unmarked birds, a prerogative dating back to the twelfth century when swan was a valuable source of meat, and any marked birds are deemed to belong to one of two Livery Companies, the Vintners and the Dyers. This means the Swanmarker has never actually marked a swan, of course, and indeed the ceremony was cancelled in 2012 due to flooding, the first time this has happened.

Dating back to the 1150s, the **Queen's Remembrancer**, the oldest judicial appointment in the country, oversees the payment of ancient 'Quit Rents'. These are payable each year at the Exchequer Court – so-called as the rent would be counted out on a chequered cloth – and include: a pair of knives (one blunt, one sharp) for a parcel of land in Shropshire; 6 horseshoes and 61 nails for an old forge that once stood to the south of the Strand;

and £11 for the City's interest in 'the Towne and Borough of Southwark'. (See Chapter 21 for more on this.)

While Freemen of the City of London are allowed to carry swords in the Square Mile (see Chapter 17), there is only one **Swordbearer of London**, who is based at the Mansion House. Another medieval appointment, this was first described in 1419 when it was established that the Lord Mayor should have 'at his own expense' someone to carry his sword before him. 'A well-bred man and one who knows how in all places, in that which unto such service pertains, to support the honour of his Lord and of the City.' The Swordbearer is supplied with a fur or Muscovy hat for his term in office, containing a pocket to safeguard the Seal of the City of London.

BIZARRE THINGS INSURED BY LLOYD'S OF LONDON

The **taste buds** of restaurant critic Egon Ronay in 1957 for £250,000.

The **fingers** of Harvey Lowe who won London's 1932 Yo-Yo World Championships and went on to teach the Prince of Wales how to do it; and Keith Richards of the Rolling Stones.

The **legs** of *Riverdance* star Michael Flatley, who reportedly insured them for £30 million at the height of his career.

A **grain of rice** was insured for £12,500; the single grain was decorated with a microscopic portrait of the Queen and Prince Philip.

Comics Abbott and Costello paid for a £250,000 insurance

policy to cover their **good humour**, providing them with a secure future if they ever argued and fell out so badly that they could no longer work as a double act.

In the 1980s, Australian cricketer Mervyn Hughes insured his 'trademark' **moustache** against loss or damage. (Tom Jones is similarly rumoured to have insured his chest hair.)

The owners of Cutty Sark whisky once offered £1 million to anyone who could capture the **Loch Ness Monster**, and insured themselves just in case anyone did. (Similar cover was taken out by the makers of the TV quiz *Who Wants to be a Millionaire?* on which there have been five millionaire winners in the UK.)

The comedian Ken Dodd insured his **teeth** for an astonishing £4.5 million.

The **voices** of Bob Dylan, the Beatles and Bruce Springsteen are all known to have been insured at some point during their careers.

The publishers of a book about Princess Anne and Captain Mark Phillips took out a policy protecting them against the royal couple **breaking up** in case the couple changed their minds ahead of publication.

The actor Jimmy 'Schnozzle' Durante insured his best-known feature – his **nose**.

Mindful it can go at any time, Bette Davis insured her **waistline** against sudden, unexpected expansion.

In the 1960s, the world's second captive **killer whale**, Namu – the first was a female called Moby Doll – was insured for his purchase price of $8,000. (It wasn't enough – at his new home in Seattle, Namu would eat 400 lb of salmon at a sitting.)

The world's largest **cigar** – 12½ ft long, 315 hours in the making and comprising 15,903 tobacco leaves – would reportedly take 339 days and nights to smoke, and was insured just in case anyone put a match to it.

The Worst Business Decisions Ever Made in London

Decca and the Beatles

Decca's Mike Smith and Dick Rowe famously signed Brian Poole and the Tremeloes instead of the Beatles. They declared, 'Not to mince words, Mr Epstein, but we don't like your boys' sound. Groups are out . . . four-piece groups with guitars particularly are finished.' The Fab Four have so far sold more than a billion records with EMI (see below) and Brian hasn't.

British Airways and Margaret Thatcher

In the 1990s, BA spent a fortune devising new 'ethnic' tail-fin designs and painting out the Union Flags on its fleet in the belief that these offended foreign passengers. The Prime Minister immediately indicated her displeasure at the move, with publicity-hungry rival Virgin grabbing hundreds of column inches by painting flags on its own aircraft. BA eventually executed a U-turn.

Royal Mail and Consignia

In 2002, an outfit called Dragon Brands somehow persuaded the 350-year-old Royal Mail to adopt an entirely meaningless name. Labour minister Stephen Byers approved the expensive change, but the public hated it and pundits were soon suggesting 'consignia' sounded like the Spanish for lost luggage. It was also pointed out, at a time when the future of the Post Office was in doubt, that Consignia plc was an unfortunate anagram of 'panic closing'. The name, inevitably, was soon switched back.

Baring Brothers and Nick Leeson

Britain's oldest merchant bank, the archetype of a venerable City institution, after more than 230 years in business Baring Brothers came crashing to the ground when its 'rogue trader' was jailed for his part in the £860-million collapse. A shocking tale of bad deals, secret accounts and a lack of oversight by bank bosses, the mid-1990s saga has since been repeated several times elsewhere and on an even larger scale.

GEC and Marconi

For years, a cash-rich behemoth headquartered in Magnet House, Kingsway, GEC was cautiously guided by the shrewd, defensive Lord Weinstock to become Britain's largest private employer. Unfortunately, the moment he stepped down, the new guys decided to buy Marconi, rebranding and 're-engineering' a large and successful business and abandoning what its managers and staff knew best. The timing could not have been worse, and, after the dot.com bubble burst in 2000, a company that at its peak had been worth £35 billion was sold for just over £1 billion.

EMI and Guy Hands

Ex-Goldman Sachs, ex-Nomura and, briefly, Britain's largest pub landlord, tax exile and buyout-baron, Guy Hands spent billions buying EMI in 2007 before suing his bank over claims that it had tricked him into paying too much for the ailing music giant. The courts disagreed, however, and, when the dust settled, more than a hundred years of recorded-music history was broken up, sold on and scattered to the winds.

Made in London – Surprisingly Old Inventions

Fax Machine

One of several pioneers working in the field of telephotography – or should that be phototelegraphy? – physicist Shelford Bidwell made his first 'scanning phototelegraph' in 1881. By 1908, similar equipment had been used to send the authorities in London a photograph of a criminal who had gone on the run, and in November 1924, a photograph of President Calvin Coolidge sent from New York to London became the first photograph to be reproduced by transoceanic radio facsimile.

Airship

It takes nothing away from the Frenchman Jules Henri Giffard, but the first powered flight by an airship was made here in England using a scale model manufactured by Thomas Monck Mason. Powered by clockwork propellers, and 13 ft long, the spindle-shaped craft first took to the air in 1834 and was later put on display at the Lowther Arcade in the Strand.

Street Lighting

The first street in the world to be lit by gas, from June 1807 Pall Mall was artificially illuminated using pipes made from old musket barrels to withstand the pressure of the coal gas. The installation was intended to celebrate King George III's birthday, and decorative gas mantles are still to be seen in the street today outside the Royal Automobile Club.

Manufactured Water

Having discovered what he called 'inflammable air' or hydrogen in 1766, the honourable, Hackney-educated Henry Cavendish (see Chapter 11) successfully synthesised water at his private laboratory on Clapham Common by exploding his inflammable air in the presence of oxygen.

Ice-Rink

A sad loss for London, the world's first artificially frozen ice-rink was the Glaciarium, which opened in 1844 in King Street, Covent Garden. Landscaped with a panorama of Lake Lucerne, it was an expensive day out – with entry charged at 1*s*. for spectators and an extra shilling for anyone wishing to skate – but a huge improvement on previous rinks, which, in place of ice, had used a rather disgusting combination of lard and salt.

Jigsaw

As long ago as 1766, London engraver John Spilsbury created what he called 'dissected maps'. As a means of entertaining and educating children, they caught on almost immediately, and very soon his company was hand-cutting maps of the world, Europe, Asia, Africa, America, England, Wales, Ireland and Scotland.

Despite their popularity, he continued in his other, more serious work, and several Spilsbury engravings are on display in the National Portrait Gallery.

Plastic

The world's first plastic was manufactured in East London and patented in 1856. Called Parkesine, after its inventor Alexander Parkes, a tendency to explode means it was less successful – and is now somewhat less well known – than its Belgian rival, Bakelite.

Roller Skates

These, too, were invented by a Belgian, John Joseph Merlin, an 'ingenious mechanick' who spent much of his life living in London. Demonstrating his skill in 1760 at a ball in Soho Square, he rocketed into the ballroom playing the violin and seriously injured himself by crashing into a large mirror. (This was valued by its owner at £500, to which can be added a couple of zeros to allow for inflation.)

Home Video

Manufactured by Major Radiovision of Wigmore Street in 1934, and on sale by mail order from Selfridges for 7*s.* each (35p), flat 10-in Radiovision discs could store 12 minutes of programming to be played back *for private use only* at 78 rpm.

Flushing Loo

In 1596, Queen Elizabeth's godson Sir John Harington published a paper called *A New Discourse of a Stale Subject, Called the Metamorphosis of Ajax*, which described a new type of loo which he had devised. He kindly installed one for Her Majesty's personal use at Richmond Palace, but the monarch declined to use it as she didn't like the noise it made.

WEIRD, WONDERFUL . . . AND USELESS

Anti-Seasick Ship

A resident of Denmark Hill, the otherwise highly successful Victorian entrepreneur Sir Henry Bessemer conceived the good ship SS *Bessemer* to counteract the normal rolling motion caused by the sea. It did this by suspending a huge weight beneath the main saloon so that passengers stayed upright as the ship rolled from side to side. It sounded good, and a mock-up worked well enough on land, but once at sea the prototype proved impossible to steer and crashed into the pier at Calais.

New and Improved Parachute

In 1837, at Vauxhall Gardens on the south bank of the Thames, Robert Cocking demonstrated his new and improved parachute by ascending in a balloon to 5,000 ft and jumping out. With thousands gathered below to see him in action, it quickly became apparent that his new design didn't work. Cocking's parachute failed to open, and he died shortly after hitting the ground.

Atmospheric Railway

Romanticised by the Victorians as an 'invisible rope of air', an experimental version of London's first atmospheric railway opened on Wormwood Scrubs in 1840. This used air pressure in sealed pneumatic tubes to suck and blow the trains along, but unfortunately when the idea was taken up by the London & Croydon Railway, it failed when rats chewed their way through the leather seals and it lost suction.

Cable Railway

For the London and Blackwall Railway running into Fenchurch Street, Robert Stephenson of *Rocket* fame mounted powerful steam engines at either end of the line and planned to pull the trains back and forth using fourteen miles of hemp rope. Unfortunately, the latter wore out with incredible regularity, and the steel cable replacements proved liable to kink. The service was subsequently abandoned, although the same line is still used today and forms part of the Docklands Light Railway (DLR).

Romance-o-Meter

Sir Francis Galton (see Chapter 11) set out to measure how much his dinner guests fancied each other. He did this by fitting pressure gauges to the legs of his dining room chairs. The idea was to measure the extent to which one guest leaned towards or away from his companions, and thus quantify the degree to which they were attracted to each other.

Basic English

In the 1920s, Charles Kay Ogden, the founder of the Orthological Institute in Bloomsbury's Gordon Square, convinced himself that the reason countries went to war was because they couldn't understand what the other side was saying. His solution was to invent Basic English, a language designed to be so simple that even a foreigner could understand it. With a total vocabulary of just 850 words

– compared to around 60,000 for an intelligent graduate – it sounded like a non-starter, and so it proved to be.

The Urinette

Following complaints that women had to pay to use cubicles but men could pee for free, the London Public Health Committee came up with its answer in 1927. 'Known as the urinette,' the official announcement read, 'it is similar to a WC but is narrower and has a flushing rim.' Unfortunately, women were soon said to be using them in 'an uncleanly manner' and the eight London boroughs that had adopted them got rid of them just as quickly.

Uphill Struggle

Frustrated at the kinetic energy lost as heat when braking, in 1899 a cyclist from Upper Norwood called James Lauder conceived a means of storing energy that could be gradually released when extra oomph was needed to go uphill. Pedalling increased the air pressure in a central cylinder, a valve then allowing this energy to be released into a pair of oscillating cylinders fitted over the front wheel when required. Unfortunately, this made the bike much harder to pedal, doubly so as the bike was so much heavier than its rivals.

What is the Livery?

The Livery is made up of the ancient trade associations of the City of London. Originally, these were simple guilds established to protect the rights of their members (while ensuring the quality of their products and services) and many trace their origins back to early medieval times.

Now overwhelmingly social, a number nevertheless continue to play an active role in the relevant industry sector and their role in the City remains highly significant. With important landholdings still belonging to the Livery, voting rights are also restricted to liverymen when it comes to electing a new Lord Mayor each year (see Chapter 21 on Ceremonial London).

Despite an adherence to tradition, the Livery continues to grow, however, and, as the names towards the end of the list suggest, new companies are still being established. It is also the case that many members of the older companies continue to be drawn from professionals within the relevant trades, or their modern equivalents. (There are, for example, still carriage-makers in the Worshipful Company of Coachmakers and Coach Harness Makers, with other Liverymen and Freemen of the same company active in the automotive and aeronautical industries.)

Livery Companies' Order of Precedence

1. The Worshipful Company of Mercers
2. The Worshipful Company of Grocers
3. The Worshipful Company of Drapers
4. The Worshipful Company of Fishmongers
5. The Worshipful Company of Goldsmiths
6. (or 7) The Worshipful Company of Skinners*
7. (or 6) The Worshipful Company of Merchant Taylors*
8. The Worshipful Company of Haberdashers
9. The Worshipful Company of Salters
10. The Worshipful Company of Ironmongers
11. The Worshipful Company of Vintners
12. The Worshipful Company of Clothworkers
13. The Worshipful Company of Dyers
14. The Worshipful Company of Brewers
15. The Worshipful Company of Leathersellers
16. The Worshipful Company of Pewterers

17. The Worshipful Company of Barbers-Surgeons
18. The Worshipful Company of Cutlers
19. The Worshipful Company of Bakers
20. The Worshipful Company of Wax Chandlers
21. The Worshipful Company of Tallow Chandlers
22. The Worshipful Company of Armourers and Brasiers
23. The Worshipful Company of Girdlers
24. The Worshipful Company of Butchers
25. The Worshipful Company of Saddlers
26. The Worshipful Company of Carpenters
27. The Worshipful Company of Cordwainers
28. The Worshipful Company of Painter-Stainers
29. The Worshipful Company of Curriers
30. The Worshipful Company of Masons
31. The Worshipful Company of Plumbers
32. The Worshipful Company of Innholders
33. The Worshipful Company of Founders
34. The Worshipful Company of Poulters
35. The Worshipful Company of Cooks
36. The Worshipful Company of Coopers
37. The Worshipful Company of Tylers and Bricklayers
38. The Worshipful Company of Bowyers
39. The Worshipful Company of Fletchers
40. The Worshipful Company of Blacksmiths
41. The Worshipful Company of Joiners and Ceilers
42. The Worshipful Company of Weavers
43. The Worshipful Company of Woolmen
44. The Worshipful Company of Scriveners
45. The Worshipful Company of Fruiterers
46. The Worshipful Company of Plaisterers
47. The Worshipful Company of Stationers and Newspaper Makers
48. The Worshipful Company of Broderers
49. The Worshipful Company of Upholders

50. The Worshipful Company of Musicians
51. The Worshipful Company of Turners
52. The Worshipful Company of Basketmakers
53. The Worshipful Company of Glaziers and Painters of Glass
54. The Worshipful Company of Horners
55. The Worshipful Company of Farriers
56. The Worshipful Company of Paviors
57. The Worshipful Company of Loriners
58. The Worshipful Society of Apothecaries
59. The Worshipful Company of Shipwrights
60. The Worshipful Company of Spectacle Makers
61. The Worshipful Company of Clockmakers
62. The Worshipful Company of Glovers
63. The Worshipful Company of Feltmakers
64. The Worshipful Company of Framework Knitters
65. The Worshipful Company of Needlemakers
66. The Worshipful Company of Gardeners
67. The Worshipful Company of Tin Plate Workers
68. The Worshipful Company of Wheelwrights
69. The Worshipful Company of Distillers
70. The Worshipful Company of Pattenmakers
71. The Worshipful Company of Glass Sellers
72. The Worshipful Company of Coachmakers and Coach Harness Makers
73. The Worshipful Company of Gunmakers
74. The Worshipful Company of Gold and Silver Wyre Drawers
75. The Worshipful Company of Makers of Playing Cards
76. The Worshipful Company of Fanmakers
77. The Worshipful Company of Carmen
78. The Honourable Company of Master Mariners
79. The City of London Solicitors' Company
80. The Worshipful Company of Farmers
81. The Guild of Air Pilots and Air Navigators

82. The Worshipful Company of Tobacco Pipe Makers and Tobacco Blenders
83. The Worshipful Company of Furniture Makers
84. The Worshipful Company of Scientific Instrument Makers
85. The Worshipful Company of Chartered Surveyors
86. The Worshipful Company of Chartered Accountants in England and Wales
87. The Worshipful Company of Chartered Secretaries and Administrators
88. The Worshipful Company of Builders Merchants
89. The Worshipful Company of Launderers
90. The Worshipful Company of Marketors
91. The Worshipful Company of Actuaries
92. The Worshipful Company of Insurers
93. The Worshipful Company of Arbitrators
94. The Worshipful Company of Engineers
95. The Worshipful Company of Fuellers
96. The Worshipful Company of Lightmongers
97. The Worshipful Company of Environmental Cleaners
98. The Worshipful Company of Chartered Architects
99. The Worshipful Company of Constructors
100. The Worshipful Company of Information Technologists
101. The Worshipful Company of World Traders
102. The Worshipful Company of Water Conservators
103. The Worshipful Company of Firefighters
104. The Worshipful Company of Hackney Carriage Drivers
105. The Worshipful Company of Management Consultants
106. The Worshipful Company of International Bankers
107. The Worshipful Company of Tax Advisers
108. The Worshipful Company of Security Professionals

*A longstanding dispute over precedence means these two companies alternate each year, an arrangement that is said to have given rise to the expression 'at sixes and sevens' although this, too, is disputed.

LONDON'S OLDEST WORKER?

Making regular appearances on local TV news programmes, French-born Pierre Jean 'Buster' Martin (1906–2011) frequently boasted about being London's oldest employee and famously went in to work at Pimlico Plumbers on the day of his 100th birthday.

Unfortunately, most of his claims have since proved impossible to verify, including his date of birth and the fact that he gained his nickname after punching a priest on the nose when he was only three years old.

In 2008, for example, he insisted that he had completed the London Marathon, but in the absence of any proof of this from the organisers, bookmakers William Hill declined to pay out £13,300 when Martin failed to produce a valid birth certificate. He was also denied an entry in the *Guinness Book of World Records*, on the grounds that he was almost certainly ninety-four at the time and not – as he claimed – 101.

14
Boozy London

'I went out drinking for about seventy hours here in London. At the end, I knew I was done.'

Gary Oldman

For all the millions who have come to know London's familiar face, like any truly great city it retains its secrets. For every Hampton Court or Westminster Abbey there are many hundreds of lesser treasures, so many indeed that the sheer weight of cultural and architectural wealth can be so overwhelming that many visitors stroll through the streets without even noticing so many fascinating buildings.

That literally thousands of these are open to the public – more than this, they positively welcome visitors, all day and half the night, and without charging even a penny to enter – makes missing the best of them sadder still.

The treasures in question are, of course, London's historic pubs, an estimated 7,000 of them all told. Of course, not all of them are that special, but with the oldest dating back to as long ago as the thirteenth century, they range widely in appearance and character from simple locals or tiny spit-and-sawdust sorts of places – some still no more than bare boards and beer barrels – through larger, positively labyrinthine coaching inns to plush, cut-glass Victorian gin palaces.

Inevitably, dating them accurately poses all sorts of problems (see below) and many claims to antiquity cheerfully ignore the fact that the building itself has been rebuilt as many times as it has served hot dinners.

Inevitably, a good few these days have embraced multiculturalism, too, so that where once the only alternative seemed to be Irish pubs, Londoners have more recently been treated to the likes of the Glassy Junction in Southall, the capital's first Punjabi pub and almost certainly the only one in the capital to accept rupees. There's also Zeitgeist, offering German food served by German staff accompanied by German beers – more than a dozen on draught and three times that number in bottles – and German soccer relayed via a big screen. (Inevitably, it is known to its regulars as the '*Wunderbar*'.)

The most famous of all, perhaps, is Soho's French House. Originally called the York Minster, and a popular 1960s Soho haunt of writers and artists, the pub sells more Ricard than any bar in London – but only half pints of beer except on April Fool's Day. Its nickname, incidentally – the locals originally referring to it as 'The French', but now formally adopted – derives from Gaston Berlemont, its most celebrated licensee, although actually he was Belgian.

Even without such exotics as these, however, one is still left with as rich an assortment as you could wish for. Architecturally, London's pubs are as cheerfully diverse as the city beyond their walls and many like the few described here are real gems, some in their own way as interesting historically as many of the capital's more traditional attractions and the best of them still able to provide a rare and unspoiled glimpse of old London – as well, of course, as first-class food and refreshment.

MAKE MINE A DOUBLE –
LONDON'S MOST EXPENSIVE SNIFTER

In October 2012, London barman Salvatore Calabrese, formerly of Duke's Hotel, St James's, broke the record for the world's most expensive cocktail with his 'Playboy Club Salvatore's Legacy' ringing the till at £5,500 a shot.

According to the *Evening Standard*, the costly concoction comprised a number of centuries-old spirits, including 1778 Clos de Griffier Vieux Çognac, 1770 Kummel Liqueur, Dubb Orange Curacao (circa 1860) and two dashes of Angostura bitters from around 1900.

The previous record, held by Dubai's Skyview Bar at the Burj Al Arab Hotel, would have set you back a paltry £3,766.52.

Hot or cold, at its best pub food is still simple, but that can mean good and affordable, often significantly more affordable than the mass of plasticky, portion-controlled fast-food and franchised outlets to which visitors frequently have to resort if they are looking for good value. Quality varies, clearly, but the dread days of margarine and stale, mousetrap cheese are now all but gone and, in central London, real cooking rarely comes cheaper than this. Just as importantly, only a very few restaurants (and positively no chains) can match the fascinating histories and evocative atmosphere of these ancient hostelries and alehouses.

Any sense of romance makes it hard not to reflect, as you take your seat in the Chop House at the back of Fleet Street's remarkable and quite unspoilt Ye Olde Cheshire Cheese, that Dickens himself once did as you do now before writing it up in his *Tale of Two Cities*. And Thameside pubs such as the old Anchor Bankside and the famous Prospect of Whitby command fantastic panoramic views across the Thames. The Anchor was used by both Pepys and Samuel Johnson, himself a friend of the Thrales who at that time owned the brewery next door. The Prospect of Whitby, once a popular hangout of river pirates and smugglers, was likewise a favourite watering hole of the notorious hanging judge, George Jeffreys, a notable imbiber.

These historical associations run deep. Further east in Rotherhithe, the Mayflower for years held a unique licence to sell British and American postage stamps thanks to its long ties with the former colony whose Pilgrim Fathers set off from the pub's back steps. Similarly, despite (or perhaps because of) its proximity to the House of Commons, Whitehall's Silver Cross is still licensed as a brothel because no one has seen fit to revoke the licence granted by Charles I. And Mayfair's strangely named 'I Am the Only Running Footman' was formerly the Running Horse, but was changed in the 1770s by its owner, the 4th Duke of Queensbury, in honour of his own manservant who was said to be able to keep up a respectable 8 mph.

DRINKS WITH SOLID ORIGINS

Champagne

The French would have you believe the drink was the creation of a Benedictine monk, and it is true that from the 1670s onwards the much-storied Dom Perignon made some significant contributions to the refermenting process that gives Champagne its sparkle.

But while he was still a young novitiate, Christopher Merret back in England had already demonstrated the process and, as long ago as 1662, had described it in a paper called *Some Observations Concerning the Ordering of Wines,* which he presented to a meeting of the Royal Society at Gresham College in Bishopsgate. (At around the same time, it was also English ingenuity, in the person of Admiral Sir Robert Mansell, which devised the means of constructing glass bottles strong enough to withstand the pressure resulting from so many bubbles.)

Buck's Fizz

A refreshing mix of Champagne and orange juice (with an optional dash of grenadine), this popular wedding cocktail and breakfast tipple is thought to have been devised by the barman at the Mayfair club of the same name. (In the early days of motoring, the Royal Automobile Club also had its own cocktail, Fred Fraeck's 1914 R.A.C., but with unfortunate associations of drink-driving this gin-and-vermouth mix is now less well known.)

John Collins

Somewhat edged out by the American Tom Collins, the original was created in the early nineteenth century by the eponymous barman at Limmer's Hotel on the corner of Conduit Street and St George Street. His base was '*genièvre*' or London Dry gin, but, in the years since, the drink has spawned a family of regional variations including a Sandy Collins (whisky), a Pierre Collins (cognac) and a rum-based Pedro Collins.

Predating almost all of London's ancient alehouses, though, is the venerable Hoop and Grapes in Aldgate, said to have origins dating back to the 1200s. It is also reputed to have a tunnel (now lost or maybe blocked) leading to the Tower.

As early as 1390, there was a Boar's Head on Eastcheap in the City (sadly, this was demolished in 1831); and The Guinea Grill just off New Bond Street is known to have first served a brew back in 1423.

But, generally, the best of the really old London pubs are those of the seventeenth century, like the aforementioned Cheshire Cheese, the George on Borough High Street and the Lamb & Flag in Covent Garden, each characterised by old varnish and creaking joists, pleasantly blackened, panelled walls, often open fires in winter and bare floorboards. Invariably dark and somewhat stark, but cosy with it, they have an ambience that positively reeks of old pewter mugs, serving wenches and navy press gangs.

They have stories to tell, too, and often of storytellers. The Lamb & Flag, for example, was for years better known as The Bucket of Blood, so ferocious were the many prize-fights staged on the premises. (In 1679, when poet laureates still frequented pubs, John Dryden was attacked and beaten here after writing scurrilous lines about the Duchess of Portsmouth, Charles II's mistress.) The George, London's last surviving galleried inn and now in the care of the National Trust, was similarly known to Shakespeare and, in the summer, strolling players still perform his works in the charming courtyard outside.

GINTERLUDE – MOTHER'S RUIN

The name 'gin' derives from Geneva (itself a corruption of the old French, '*genièvre*', meaning juniper) but the drink's earliest origins are to be found in the Netherlands where the Dutch first distilled grain and flavoured it lightly with piquant juniper berries and other botanicals. The English – and Londoners in particular – developed a taste for the resulting liquor early on, with its popularity being further encouraged around 1690 by soldiers returning home from the Duke of Marlborough's campaigns.

It is most famous, of course, as the fabled 'Mother's Ruin' of times past – two of William Hogarth's best-loved engravings contrast the cheerfully bucolic scenes of innocuous *Beer Street* with the seedy, ruinous degradation of sinister *Gin Lane*. The drink's popularity among the capital's drinking classes owed much to its low price, the result of some ill-considered laws introduced by William of Orange in a bid to discourage the buying of imported spirits.

With gin, it was said at the time, one could get drunk for a penny and dead drunk for two. The stuff was soon unlicensed, rarely taxed and on sale everywhere, from barbers' shops to street barrows. With more than 15,000 outlets in total, including an estimated one in seven private houses in the East End, Londoners soon had plenty of opportunities to avail themselves. Unsurprisingly, annual consumption rose rapidly in the 1730s, doubling in quantity to 6½ million gallons in less than a decade. Suspecting that drinking on this scale encouraged not just drunkenness but also idleness and vice 'in the inferior sort of people', Parliament eventually moved to raise the duty payable with a new Gin Act in 1751.

It took almost a century for the drink's image to recover, even so. With the Royal Navy carrying Angostura bitters as a preventive medicine on its voyages around the Empire, ships' officers quickly recognised that, by using the medicine as a sophisticated mixer, the resulting pink gin or 'pinkers' made a nice change from standard-issue naval grog or rum.

Colonial hands in the Indian subcontinent were meanwhile making discoveries of their own, namely that tonic water containing quinine – widely prescribed as a measure against malaria – went rather well with it, too. Before long, the idea of drinking gin and tonic had travelled back home and, once again, it caught on immediately.

Despite this somewhat chequered history, London or Dry Gin has long maintained a reputation for particular quality. The aptly named Beefeater is the last of the big names actually to produce gin in the capital, however, from its distillery close to Kennington Oval.

Other pubs have a more gruesome tale to tell, however, such as the Grenadier in Wilton Row just off Belgrave Square. With its distinctive kerbside sentry box and martial decorations, it is believed by many to be haunted by the ghost of a young guards officer who was caught cheating at cards and summarily flogged to death in the cellar by his fellow subalterns.

The story could just be a colourful local legend, of course, but the Blind Beggar in the East End is definitely the place where Ronnie Kray shot dead a rival gang member called George Cornell. (The year was 1966 and the jukebox was playing 'The Sun Ain't Gonna Shine Anymore' by the Walker Brothers.) Similarly, it is well documented that the Anglesea Arms in South Kensington was chosen by Bruce Reynolds for a preliminary meeting to discuss the feasibility of mounting what was to become the Great Train Robbery.

Perhaps the most touching of these old pub yarns, however, is that of the Widow's Son in Bow where, once a year, a sailor ceremonially hangs a hot cross bun over the bar in a ritual dating back more than two centuries. In so doing, he commemorates a real widow who, expecting her sailor son home for Easter, kept a warm bun for him. Sadly, he never returned, but each year until her death she added another bun to the mouldering, blackened bundle hanging above the bar, the same bundle that is preserved and honoured today by the locals in this perfect example of a traditional, early Victorian East End pub.

Less believable, perhaps, is the suggestion that Dr Johnson wrote sections of his famous dictionary while seated in the Cheshire Cheese. Certainly, Boswell refuses to confirm it but it is an enduring myth and, sitting in its characterful gloom with sawdust still on the floor, it is easy to imagine the good doctor (whose house is in nearby Gough Square) mulling over the perfect definition. Its entrance hidden away in Wine Office Court, a narrow alleyway off Fleet Street where once the city's wine sellers came to obtain their warrants to trade, the present pub has long been a favourite of writers and journalists. It rose from the ashes of the Great Fire only as recently as 1667, but the cellars are much older and incorporate part of the undercroft of a 600-year-old Carmelite monastery. So, too, is the front step, now worn thin by hundreds of years and thousands of feet and so protected by an iron grille.

Sitting astride a busy junction of road, river and rail a little further to the west, there is little on the approach to prepare one for the strange and wonderful wedge-shaped Black Friar. Outside stands a statue of a jolly monk, set above a mosaic and beaming down on passers-by; inside, it is a veritable riot of Art Nouveau with creamy, rich-veined marble walls and archways, hand-beaten Arts and Crafts copper murals depicting more jolly friars enjoying themselves, gleaming gold leaf on the ceiling, inglenooks and open fireplaces with burnished brass firedogs and everywhere strange admonishing slogans and bon mots preserved in the stonework: 'Finery is Foolery' – 'Haste is Slow' – 'A Good Thing is Soon Snatched Up'. It is all quite delightful.

In the 1960s, a group of speculators wished to pull the old place down so they could develop the site, but the public outcry (led by another poet laureate, Sir John Betjeman) was enormous and, thankfully, today a preservation order has secured the Black Friar for all of us. That such a special place could have been lost seems incredible now, for with its decor as golden and as grand in its way as the Ritz, it is a unique adornment to the area.

At the Red Lion in Duke of York Street, this seventeenth-century simplicity gives way to the nineteenth century's taste for over-decoration in a diminutive but charming and utterly authentic example of a classic Victorian gin palace. Its lush, plush pub interior is the best in St James's, with elaborately carved and deeply polished mahogany, etched glass panels and gleaming cut-glass mirrors, and a genuine 'Lincrusta' or embossed decorated paper ceiling. Most obviously, it imparts to this rare period survivor precisely the sort of atmosphere a thousand 'repro-Victoriana' pubs have signally failed to capture, and on a more intimate scale than the more famous Princess Louise, another period gem so admired for its high Victorian style that even the urinals have been listed by English Heritage as worthy of preservation.

Sadly, many London pubs have disappeared in recent years – at the time of writing, the current loss is reckoned to be as many as six a week – but the best look likely to survive. Few these days are mere boozers – a vulgar derivation of the Middle-English '*bousen*', incidentally, thieves' slang for drinking to excess – and the best are perfect capsules of London life: as individual and as characterful as their customers, and as historic as any of London's great attractions.

Where to Find Them – Britain's Best Pub Crawl

The Anchor Bankside, Park Street, Southwark, SE1
The Anglesea Arms, Selwood Terrace, SW7
The Black Friar, Queen Victoria Street, EC4
The Blind Beggar, Whitechapel Road, E1

The French House, Dean Street, W1
The George Inn, Borough High Street, SE1
Glassy Junction, South Road, Southall, UB1
The Grenadier, Wilton Row, Belgravia, SW1
I Am the Only Running Footman, Charles Street, Mayfair, W1
The Lamb & Flag, Rose Street, Covent Garden, WC2
The Mayflower, Rotherhithe Street, SE16
The Princess Louise, High Holborn, WC1
The Prospect of Whitby, Wapping Wall, E1
The Red Lion, Duke of York Street, St James's, W1
The Widow's Son, Devons Road, E3
Ye Olde Cheshire Cheese, Fleet Street, EC4
Zeitgeist, Black Prince Road, SE11

London's Oldest Boozer?

Often debated – something that is best done over a pint – perhaps the best that can be said is that more than a few London pubs can trace their origins (if not what remains of their architecture) back to 1500 and beyond. Some we've already heard about, and here are a few more in no particular order:

The White Hart, Drury Lane, WC2

With 'roots' in 1216, the White Hart claims to be the 'oldest licensed premises in London' and numbers Dick Turpin among its erstwhile regulars. (Turpin was born in a pub, of course, as his dad had one out at Hempstead in Essex.)

The Red Lion, Whitehall, SW1

The Prime Minister's local has been the closest pub to Downing Street for years, but predates the street (which was laid out in the 1680s) by a good 250 years. Occasionally, PMs are snapped with a pint in hand, an attempt to appear like they're one of the lads, but rarely this close to home. (A working facsimile of the pub is also rumoured to have been installed in a secret Cold War-era government bunker in Wiltshire, somewhere for civil servants to relax during the Third World War, but this has not proved possible to verify.)

The Cittie of Yorke, High Holborn, WC1

A pub has been on this site since around 1430 and, although the present building is Grade II-listed, the Tudor façade is decidedly *faux* and dates from no earlier than the 1920s.

Prospect of Whitby, Wapping Wall, E1

With early sixteenth-century origins, the aforementioned Prospect claims to be the oldest surviving riverside tavern and takes its name from a vessel that frequently tied up outside. Artists such as Whistler and Turner painted views from the tavern, and Londoners came here en route to see pirates hanged at Execution Dock. But the building iteslf is certainly not that old, as the original was almost entirely destroyed in a nineteenth-century fire.

Ye Olde Mitre, Ely Place, EC1

The hardest pub to find in London traces its history back to 1546 when it was built by the Bishop of Ely for his servants. It is popularly but erroneously said to be in Cambridgeshire, not London, because the bishops had their palace nearby and claimed the land for themselves.

The Grapes, Narrow Street, E14

Established no later than 1583, and a rare Blitz survivor,

Narrow Street also avoided being swept away during the docklands developments of the 1980s and the pub now offers one of the best views of the river. It is owned by actor Sir Ian McKellen and a couple of chums.

The Seven Stars, Carey Street, WC2

Popular with lawyers as well as tourists – the Inns of Court are nearby, as well as the Royal Courts – the lovely Seven Stars celebrated its 400th anniversary in 2002.

The George Inn Yard, Borough High Street, SE1

Famously the last galleried coaching inn in London, and now part of the National Trust. Rebuilt in 1667, and still highly atmospheric, it has part of the old stabling yard remaining and occasionally Shakespeare's plays are performed outside.

The Old Bell Tavern, Fleet Street, EC4

Supposedly built by Sir Christopher Wren for masons working on the nearby St Bride's church, the building itself is at least 300 years old, although the likelihood is that pre-Fire another tavern occupied the same site.

The Lamb, Lamb's Conduit Street, WC1

Built in the 1720s, the pub takes its name from philanthropist William Lamb who provided a conduit to supply the area with relatively clean, fresh water. Its delightful interior, unique in London, features etched glass 'snob screens' to enable guilt-ridden drinkers to remain out of sight, and it boasts what is almost certainly London's oldest working jukebox.

15

Private London

'When it's three o'clock in New York, it's still 1938 in London.'

Bette Midler

Who Owns London?

In one sense we all do – it's an authentic world city, and most of us who have lived far enough inside the M25 at some point conceive a sense of ownership. But in another, more legitimate, sense, great swathes of London are still privately owned. Admittedly, some of the largest landlords – such as the Crown Estate and the Church Commissioners – may appear to be public bodies. But even if they were (which they are not), aristocratic and family trusts still own and control a far greater proportion of what remains the most valuable land, not just in Britain, but anywhere on the planet.

A tradition of inheritance rather than sale means the precise extent of these private fiefdoms is hard if not impossible to determine, and values can only be guessed at, with prime London real estate costing as much as £100 million an acre, and rising year on year. The real surprise, perhaps, is how durable these estates have proved to be, with the names most associated with a dozen of the more valuable ones shown below underlining how nearly all of them date back literally hundreds of years. In fact, only one estate of any real size in London, centred on Soho, has been established within living memory.

Duke of Westminster	300 acres of Mayfair and Belgravia
Baron Howard de Walden	110 acres, mostly around Harley Street
Viscount Portman	110 acres, mostly around Marylebone
Earl Cadogan	90 acres, mostly in Chelsea
Mr Paul Raymond	70 acres, mostly in Soho
HRH Prince Charles	40 acres, mostly around Kennington
Viscount Petersham	29 acres, mainly around South Kensington
Duke of Bedford	20 acres, mostly in and around Bloomsbury
Marquess of Northampton	20 acres, mostly in Canonbury and Islington
Marquess of Salisbury	20 acres, much of it around Leicester Square
Duke of Norfolk	10 acres, most of it commercial property
Baron Rothschild	4 acres, much of it in the Paddington area

LONDON'S OLDEST CLUBS (AND THEIR SECRETS)

Some of central London's most historic and architecturally most important buildings are never open to the general public. With lofty Georgian and Victorian interiors, extensive art collections, elegant libraries, smoking rooms and restaurants – and, in a few cases, large gardens and even subterranean swimming pools – these are the comfortably discreet bastions of traditional London clubland.

The oldest date back literally hundreds of years and, despite jokes about old buffers and crusted port, their appeal remains as strong as ever and membership can be hard to obtain. Inevitably, some have fallen by the wayside, like the Cocoa Tree Club at 64 St James's Street, which, until 1840, had its own brothel and a good many MPs among the members. But, spacious and conservative, today's survivors seem on the whole to be in rude good health.

1693 – White's

37-38 St James's Street, SW1
Most clubs would be overjoyed by royal visits, but when Her Majesty lunched at White's – a strictly private event and a unique honour in 300 years of this emphatically all-male establishment – it was decided to hang the official photograph of the occasion in the loo.

1762 – Boodle's

28 St James's Street, SW1
For many years, the rules allowed for any member seeking to join White's to be sacked immediately, and waitresses were required to ensure their skirt hems were no more than 18 in. from the ground. The club was also the last to dispense with chamber pots, which it retained for the benefit of older members 'whose habits were formed before the days of modern sanitation'.

1764 – Brooks's

60 St James's Street, SW1
Among the club's more eccentric members, the 9th Duke of Devonshire used to sit in the entrance hall striking fellow

members he didn't like the look of with a lead-weighted walking stick. Sir Edward Elgar similarly used to require the hall porter to telephone his home in Worcestershire so he could hear his dogs barking, while the 12th Duke of St Albans frequently dropped in to have his watch wound by the staff.

1819 – Travellers'

106 Pall Mall, SW1
At its foundation, candidates had to have travelled at least 500 miles in a straight line from England, and no fewer than five of the original members – Wellington, Canning, Lord Aberdeen, Lord John Russell and Palmerston – went on to become Prime Minister. As this might suggest, the club has never enjoyed the reputation of being the most *fun*.

1824 – Athenaeum

107 Pall Mall, SW1
With a preponderance of bishops and academics among its members, the club relishes a reputation for seriousness. It was, for example, the last to install a bar (nearly a century and a half after opening) but then made the substantial error of electing a DJ as a member – Jimmy Savile, the prodigious sex-offender.

1824 – Oriental

Stratford Place, W1
Waitress Alice was employed at the club in 1916, and more than 60 years later (aged 91) she was still reporting for duty at 5.30 a.m. each morning. The club also famously retained the services of three hedgehogs in the kitchen, in an attempt to deal with an infestation of black beetle.

1830 – Oxford & Cambridge

71 Pall Mall, SW1
Until the mid-1990s, lady members – albeit Oxbridge graduates like their male counterparts – were forbidden to use the main staircase or principal library. (A shelf of romantic novels was rumoured to have been set aside for their use.)

1831 – Garrick

15 Garrick Street, WC2
Members famously blackballed Bernard Levin and Jeremy Paxman but admitted Lord Havers who, as Attorney-General during the 1987 *Spycatcher* trial, carelessly gave away details of how he planned to win the case. He did this by discussing it openly while standing at the urinals, and promptly lost.

1832 – Carlton

69 St James's Street, SW1
Because all Conservative Party leaders have enjoyed the privileges of membership, in 1975 the members effectively chose to declare Margaret Thatcher an 'honorary man' rather than change the rules to admit lady members.

1832 – City of London

19 Old Broad Street, EC2
Disgracefully, members considered selling off their elegant nineteenth-century clubhouse in the 1970s, reaping a substantial personal profit from its demolition. Fortunately, planning permission was denied them, and this potentially lucrative but philistine move was abandoned.

1836 – Reform

104-5 Pall Mall, SW1
In 1977, the smoking room echoed to the sound of monocles falling into pink gins when pictures were published in *Penthouse* magazine showing a television presenter in the club. The late Paula Yates was photographed, naked, on the staircase, in the library and on the floor of the main saloon.

1837 – Army & Navy

37 Pall Mall, SW1
The club is still known as 'the Rag' to its largely military membership because, in the early days, the quality of the food was so poor that after suffering a meal there it was described by one of its own members as a 'rag and famish affair'.

1841 – Pratt's

14 Park Place, SW1
The personal possession of the dukes of Devonshire since the 9th Duke bought it in the 1930s, this small but exclusive basement club opens only in the evenings. It has one long table that members share and, to avoid the befuddled becoming even more confused, the club servants all answer to the name George (except one waitress who is known as Georgina).

1849 – East India

16 St James's Square, SW1
At one point, the club boasted no fewer than a dozen members who had been awarded the Victoria Cross, but during the Indian Mutiny it nearly collapsed due to the

huge proportion of officers and administrators recalled to the subcontinent. Since then, having absorbed several others – including the Devonshire and Public Schools – it seems to be thriving.

1857 – Savage

1 Whitehall Place, SW1
Despite its professed modesty (the name comes from a seedy drunk, an eighteenth-century poet who was imprisoned for murder and died a pauper) and its lack of a clubhouse, the peripatetic Savage can boast that in a single year no fewer than three of its members sat on the throne of England: George V, Edward VIII and George VI.

1862 – Naval & Military

4 St James's Square, SW1
As recently as the 1950s, the club employed an ancient, one-armed Boer war veteran as a runner. Ex-Sergeant Harris was paid 6*d.* a mile to carry messages around London for his members, and to help them with their luggage.

1863 – Arts Club

40 Dover Street, W1
The club scandalised London in the nineteenth century by allowing members to play billiards on Sundays, and sacked the poet Swinburne after he lost his temper and trashed a number of members' hats by jumping up and down on them.

1868 – Savile

69 Brook Street, W1
For many years, the club continued the tradition of

sending snuff round with the port, it having been observed that many of those who survived the 1919 Spanish 'flu pandemic had partaken of both.

1868 – Turf

5 Carlton House Terrace, SW1
In 1963, the membership included more than half of Britain's dukes and, as at Boodle's, there were still four chamber pots available in various sizes for those members who preferred to use them.

1876 – Beefsteak

9 Irving Street, WC2
Around 1905, the police raided the club, a first-floor dining room off Leicester Square, thinking it was a brothel. They discovered the Prime Minister lunching with the Archbishop of Canterbury, the Lord Chancellor and the Governor of the Bank of England – and withdrew.

1882 – National Liberal

Whitehall Place, SW1
Proud of its immense clubhouse – an exuberant explosion of polished marble and encaustic tiles – in the 1920s members were annoyed to discover the Conservative Lord Chancellor using it for 'comfort breaks'. On being challenged, Lord Birkenhead claimed he had mistaken the place for a public lavatory.

1891 – Caledonian

9 Halkin Street, SW1
The club once agreed to set up a block and tackle to enable the corpse of a 24-st member to 'leave the club in

an orderly fashion' – maybe there's something in those rumours about deep-fried Mars bars north of the border after all. In the 1960s, uniquely for a London club, but unsurprisingly, it had nearly 200 members whose names began with 'Mc' or 'Mac'.

1893 – Cavalry & Guards

127 Piccadilly, W1
Great ones for stuffiness and standing on ceremony, junior officers were traditionally barred from positioning themselves in front of a fire and had to rise from their chairs whenever a superior officer entered the room. A member who found himself in court was also likely to be expelled for bringing the club into disrepute, even if he was acquitted by the jury.

1895 – City University

50 Cornhill, EC3
The club was late to grant membership to graduates of universities other than Oxford and Cambridge, but until relatively recently had one of the longest waiting lists in London despite (or perhaps because of) a longstanding refusal to admit women.

1897 – Royal Automobile

89 Pall Mall, SW1
The best-equipped club in London is also one of the least exclusive, so much so that having been tipped off by Kim Philby, spies Burgess and Maclean were able to lunch here before fleeing to Moscow and did so without being recognised.

1917 – Royal Air Force

128 Piccadilly, W1
In 1954, the committee inadvertently approved the candidature of Flying Officer J. L. Bird, only to return the subscription cheque when it emerged that Jean Bird was, in fact, a member of the Women's Royal Air Force.

London's Largest Private Gardens

Buckingham Palace – 42 acres

Very much the sovereign's private domain, limited public access is granted only very rarely, for example by invitation to one of the aforementioned Palace Garden Parties and to the occasional special jubilee event. Highlights for the fortunate few include more than 2.5 miles of gravel paths, an extensive lake fed from the Serpentine and a mulberry tree planted (for the benefit of silkworms) for James I. The celebrated 39-ton 'Waterloo Vase' was intended by Napoleon to mark his victories, but was instead presented to the Prince Regent after his defeat.

Winfield House, Regent's Park – 12 acres

Since 1955, the official residence of their ambassador to the Court of St James's, neo-Georgian Winfield House was sold to the American people for a single dollar by the Woolworth heiress Barbara Hutton. Unusually for London, many of the plants are still raised on site from seedlings, with new plantings being made at a rate of around 7,000 a year by a gardener recruited not from the USA but from Leeds Castle in Kent.

Lambeth Palace – 10 acres

The London home of the Archbishop of Canterbury for nearly 800 years, the impressive gardens at Lambeth Palace are managed by a staff of just three, one of whom is part time. Because of this, volunteers are keenly sought, which is probably the best way to gain regular access as the gardens are rarely open to the general public.

Chelsea Physic Garden – 4 acres

Britain's second-oldest botanical garden (after Oxford), this delightful, hidden enclave was established in 1673 to train apprentices of the Worshipful Society of Apothecaries (see Chapter 13). The walled garden is opened to the public on special days, a fascinating treat for horticulturalists as its warm microclimate has proved perfect for the more than 5,000 edible, medicinal and historical specimens that grow here.

Inner Temple Garden – 3 acres

Broad lawns, large plane trees and rare specimens of medlar, quince and mulberry make this quiet, riverside oasis one of the delights of central London. Though very much the private preserve of lawyers, it opens at 12.30 p.m. on most weekdays, although the public are expected to be gone by 3.00 p.m. and, if they are not, will be ushered out fairly smartly.

Aubrey House, Kensington – 2 acres

The most private of all and thus largely unknown, this large, eighteenth-century house near Holland Park was home to the 1st Earl Grosvenor – a direct ancestor of the present Duke of Westminster – and is now owned by writer, publisher and philanthropist Sigrid Rausing. The gardens are never open to the public.

16

Military London

'The bright gleam has caught the helmets of our soldiers, and warmed and cheered all our hearts.'

Sir Winston Churchill

London's Ten Biggest Bangs

In the City, the term 'Big Bang' refers to the process of financial deregulation that ushered in the yuppies during the 1980s. For London's military and civil authorities, however, it has rather different connotations, arising in large part from their own unwise habit of sanctioning munitions manufacture in built-up areas but also to London's unenviable but longstanding status as a target for terrorist groups.

SCOTS, IRISH OR WELSH – SPOT THE DIFFERENCE

Their unique ceremonial role means the officers and men of the Brigade of Guards are the most readily identifiable soldiers in the British Army, but comprising five different regiments they are also the hardest to tell one from another. To most Londoners and the vast majority of tourists, the Foot Guards all seem to wear the same delightfully anachronistic red uniforms. In fact, subtle differences on their tunics enable observers to distinguish one regiment from another, as the following table shows:

Regiment	*Buttons*	*Collar Badge*	*Bearskin Hackle**
Grenadier	Singles	Grenade	White on left side
Coldstream	Pairs	Garter star	Red on right side
Scots	Threes	Thistle star	None
Irish	Fours	Shamrock	Blue on right side
Welsh	Fives	Leek	White/green on left side

*A hackle is a clipped feather plume, and a bearskin should never, ever be referred to as a 'busby'. At the time of writing, the hats are still made using genuine black bear from official Canadian culls, but the search is on for a suitable synthetic alternative able to withstand the effects of static electricity build-up and the British weather.

1650 – All Hallows-by-the-Tower

When twenty-seven barrels of gunpowder stored in a yard next to the famous City church (see Chapters 5 and 21) exploded on 4 January, the west tower was destroyed together with around fifty houses in the area and the Rose Tavern. The death toll was conservatively estimated at sixty-seven.

1716 – Moorfields

Mr Bagley's Foundry was commissioned by the War Office to melt down a quantity of captured French cannon but, unfortunately, workmen poured the molten metal into damp moulds. The moisture caused these moulds to explode, killing Matthew Bagley, his son and fifteen of their men while injuring a number of VIPs observing the process. The horse having bolted, the extent of the carnage persuaded the government to take munitions work in-house from that point onwards and to move it out of London – in particular to Woolwich Arsenal.

1846 – Woolwich Arsenal

With the Arsenal soon taking responsibility for all British 'brass' gun manufacture (actually bronze), in 1846 the press reported that 'an explosion of the most awful character' had been reported at Woolwich, and that seven workmen had perished in the blast. Under cover of official secrecy, the cause was not revealed.

1864 – Belvedere Powder Magazines

On 1 October, two powder magazines situated on the south bank of the Thames exploded. Between them, the pair, located between Woolwich and Erith, had been used to store an estimated 52 tons of gunpowder and the blast was felt throughout London, and heard up to 50 miles away. The calamity claimed nine lives, a figure that would have been much higher had not the two magazines been built out on a relatively desolate area of marshland.

1867 – Clerkenwell House of Detention

On 13 December, the prison yard was rocked by an explosion. In an attempt to free their arms dealer and other prisoners, members of the Fenian Society had conspired to bring down the yard wall using a wheelbarrow full of explosive. A dozen people were killed, and as many as 120 injured when the blast brought down houses in Corporation Row. Several executions followed, including that of ringleader Michael Barrett, the last person to be publicly executed in London (see Chapter 1).

1874 – Regent's Park

In the early morning of 10 October, a fully laden barge from the Royal Gunpowder Mills at Waltham Abbey caught fire as it passed beneath a bridge on the Regents Canal. Before the crew could take evasive action, the *Tilbury* exploded, killing all four of them, destroying several houses (including that of Royal Academician Sir Lawrence Alma-Tadema) and several animal enclosures at the Royal Zoological Gardens. Macclesfield Bridge sustained particularly heavy damage but was then rebuilt using salvaged parts. This explains why several deep grooves worn in the support pillars by the tow-ropes of horse-drawn barges now appear to be on the wrong side. When the bridge was rebuilt a decision was taken to turn the pillars round in order to even up the wear.

1917 – Silvertown

The loudest sound ever heard in London, on 19 January a massive explosion ripped through the Brunner Mond Chemical Works in West Ham. More than 50 tons of TNT vaporised in an instant, killing 73 people and injuring more than 400. It didn't seem like it at the time, but the timing was lucky – the blast occurred at 6.52 p.m., meaning most of the workforce had left the site. It was also too early for them to have gone up to bed, which was fortunate as many of the houses in the area had their upper storeys ripped apart by the shockwave. In all, more than 900 properties were destroyed and a further 70,000 damaged, including many on the other side of the Thames. (The *New York Times* even reported that windows were blown out of the Savoy Hotel, and that a taxi had nearly toppled over in Pall Mall.)

1992 – Baltic Exchange

Three people died on 10 April when IRA bombers attacked this fine Edwardian edifice in the heart of London's financial centre. A further ninety-one city workers were injured in the detonation of more than a ton of fertiliser and Semtex plastic explosive that had been concealed in a white truck. With the cost put at £800 million – more than the cumulative total of all the other IRA explosions up to that point – the damage to the listed building was so extensive that permission was given to demolish it despite a pre-existing preservation order. Today, the site is occupied by the Gherkin, with the Exchange awaiting reconstruction in Estonia.

1993 – Bishopsgate

Another explosion less than a year later, involving another 1-ton fertiliser bomb in a tipper-truck, caused an estimated £1 billion worth of damage and affected buildings as far as 600 yards away. Casualties included the Nat West Tower, Liverpool Street Station, and the pretty little fifteenth-century church of St Ethelburga's, which collapsed amidst some 500 tons of broken glass. The latter was eventually, painstakingly, reconstructed and a security 'ring of steel' thrown up around the City to prevent such a thing happening again. Incredibly, just one person was killed, a *News of the World* photographer who had ignored warnings to get his story.

1996 – Canary Wharf

With the City protected in this way, the attention of the IRA switched to London's newest financial district in the Docklands.

In the early evening of 9 February, a third fertiliser bomb – smaller, but still deadly – exploded near South Quays Underground Station causing £100 million of damage. Two people were killed, thirty-nine injured, and South Quay Plaza was largely destroyed, leaving a crater 10 ft deep.

London's Weirdest Cold War Relics

North End Station, NW3

Nicknamed 'Bull and Bush', after the nearby pub made famous by a thousand cockney music-hall singalongs, this Tube station on the Northern Line (between Hampstead Heath and Golders Green) never saw a single passenger enter or leave a train.

Unique among London's forty or so 'ghost stations', it effectively closed before it had even opened as it became surplus to requirements following the happy collapse of an awful-sounding scheme to build suburban semis all over the Heath. In the 1950s, it was fitted out to be London Transport's emergency HQ in the event of a nuclear attack by Russia, but today all that can be seen of it above ground is an anonymous, white concrete blockhouse. This is little larger than a domestic tool shed, and is tucked away behind a fence in Hampstead Way.

RAF Kelvedon Hatch, CM14

Outside London but very much a part of it, this slightly strange-looking chalet-bungalow near Brentwood in Essex is actually the guardroom of a vast, fortified citadel built into an adjacent hillside. This was designed to shelter as many as 600 military and civilian personnel, the most senior establishment bods charged with assessing the scale of destruction after the nuclear balloon had gone up.

Now a museum (follow the slightly comical 'This way to the secret bunker' signs), it included facilities to house the PM and his Cabinet, as well as BBC staff brought over from Broadcasting House. Together, with Whitehall presumably lying in ruins, they would have provided the command HQ from which to organise and instruct any survivors in the shocking aftermath of an atomic attack.

Pear Tree House, Lunham Road, SE19

Another important Civil Defence bunker was concealed beneath an anonymous block of two-bedroom flats on the Central Hill Estate in Upper Norwood. The flats were built in the wake of the 1963 Cuban Missile Crisis on the site of a crater made by a German V-2 rocket – i.e. the direct ancestor of the intercontinental ballistic missiles that threatened to turn the Cold War hot. Somehow, the secret leaked out shortly afterwards and the supposedly bomb-proof doors were frequently plastered with CND stickers until the 1980s. Following protests from left-leaning Lambeth Borough Council – which had declared itself to be a so-called 'nuclear-free zone' around the same time – the bunker was eventually decommissioned in 1993.

Took's Court, EC4

One hundred feet beneath this narrow City alleyway, with an anonymous entrance round the corner at 39 Furnival Street, this deep-level shelter housed a giant 'atom-proof' telephone exchange. Equipped with its own sick-bay, sleeping accommodation and a canteen for up to 150 staff, it was reportedly supplied with enough food and water for a six-week shutdown.

Most significantly, the exchange also contained the famous Cold War 'hot-line', linking the Kremlin with the White House in the hope that Eisenhower and Khrushchev could engage in jaw-jaw rather than war-war. Today, the biggest giveaway to its existence is a large crane over the Furnival Street entrance, presumably used to lower heavy telecoms equipment down into the depths of the bunker.

Waterloo Siren, SE1

A favourite for cabbies to point out to tourists, an old air-raid siren can be seen on one of the railway bridges leading in to Waterloo Station. Unlikely to be of Second World War vintage – there were hundreds of these, but they were all removed after VE Day – it is assumed to have been installed to warn of an impending Soviet attack. That said, and rather disappointingly, it has more recently been suggested that it is simply there to warn Londoners the next time the Thames overflows its banks.

45 Cranley Drive, HA4

Another anonymous chalet-bungalow, this time close to RAF Northolt in suburban Ruislip. In the 1950s, it was home to a couple called Helen and Peter Kroger, in reality two American communists called Lona and Morris Cohen. For years, from 1954 to 1961, the pair transmitted 'information of special importance' from the ordinary-looking bungalow to their Soviet masters.

Part of the Portland Spy Ring, which had an interest in advanced naval technology being developed and tested on the coast of Dorset, they were eventually caught and imprisoned. In 1969, the pair were exchanged for a businessman called Gerald Brooke, who was being held by the Russians on a charge of espionage. Today, there is nothing to distinguish their house from its neighbours, although after nearly half a century its infamy is still well known to locals.

British Museum Station, WC1

Another ghost station, this time on the Central Line, although there is nothing to see of it above ground in Bury Place nor at the former entrance at what is now 133 High Holborn. The station was taken over by the Ministry of Defence following its closure in the 1930s and, for the duration of the Cold War, held by the Brigade of Guards. Beyond 'administration' it has never been explained what purpose it served, and today it is thought to be used for storage.

South East London Regional War Room, Kemnal Road, BR7

Another of London's four Civil Defence Control centres, this ugly concrete blockhouse was badly vandalised after being decommissioned and then sold to a developer in the late 1990s. After being converted into a luxurious £3-million private home – an extraordinary project with a central atrium and swimming pool – it was bought by a City financier and his family who, liking the contrast, swapped it for a medieval, timber-framed house.

17
Illegal London

'It is my belief, Watson, founded upon my experience, that the lowest and vilest alleys in London do not present a more dreadful record of sin than does the smiling and beautiful countryside.'

Sherlock Holmes in *The Copper Beeches*
by Sir Arthur Conan Doyle

Ten Infamous Highwaymen of London

Isaac Atkinson – Executed 1640

Unusual in that he was an Oxford graduate and a specialist who preferred ambushing lawyers to laymen, Atkinson took to crime as a way of supporting the lifestyle he felt he owed himself as the son of a gentleman. After a rare departure from his normal *modus operandi* – he robbed an ordinary woman at Turnham Green – Atkinson was hunted down and, despite shooting dead a number of his pursuers, was captured. 'Gentlemen,' he said on the gallows at Tyburn, 'there's nothing like a merry life, and a short one.' And then he swung.

Claude Duval – Executed 1670

The French-born Duval or Du Vall arrived in London at the Restoration, having entered the service of an English nobleman in exile. Perhaps as a consequence of his exotic continental countenance, memories of him have been much embroidered with tales – for example, that he would dance with lady victims and charge their husbands to watch. What is known is that he was run to ground in a tavern in Chandos Place, W1, and, like Atkinson, hanged at Tyburn.

Jack Collet – Executed 1691

Also known as Jack Cole, Southwark-born Collet had a thing about religion and, after a few years disguised as a bishop, he succeeded in robbing a real one. (Apprehended on the road from London to Farnham, the Bishop of Winchester was ordered to hand over his robes which Collet then appropriated to wear for his work.) He was eventually charged with 'sacrilegious burglary' after robbing the church of St Bartholomew-the-Great in June 1691, and he met his end at Tyburn shortly afterwards.

Tom Rowland – Executed 1699

Rowland was another who liked dressing up, and, after learning to ride side-saddle, he disguised himself as a woman for many of his more successful hold-ups. For eighteen years, the ruse worked a treat, but he was finally apprehended at Hounslow and sent to Newgate where – apparently – the romance of his calling meant he received many women visitors. Refusing to repent for his crimes, Rowland was carted to Tyburn for the usual.

Nathaniel Hawes – Executed 1721

A familiar figure on the roads around Hackney and Shoreditch,

Hawes famously refused to plead in court until (he said) a 'suit of fine clothes' was returned to him, which he intended to wear to the gallows. His refusal meant he was liable to be tortured, and he duly was by being pressed under a board or door on which was placed 250 lb of masonry. Eventually able to take no more, he pleaded not guilty, but no one believed him and he was hanged a few days before Christmas.

William Gordon – Executed 1733

Not much is known about Gordon's career as a highwayman, much of it spent between Epping Forest and Knightsbridge, but after his execution at Tyburn, a slightly ghoulish attempt was made to bring him back to life. Unknown to the court, a surgeon, M. Chovot, arranged to make an incision in Gordon's windpipe before he was hanged, and then to 'open a vein' after he had been cut down. Needless to say, it didn't work, although the corpse reportedly groaned once after being removed to a house in the Edgware Road.

Dick Turpin – Executed 1739

Born in Essex, trained as a butcher and hanged at York, as with Jack the Ripper there has been so much talked and written about Dick Turpin that, beyond the basics, it is hard to tell fact from fiction.

For a while, he is known to have lived at Whitechapel, and later still on Millbank, but when London became too hot for comfort he famously fled north and assumed the alias of 'Palmer'. Unfortunately for him, a letter to his brother revealed his true identity to Yorkshire magistrates, and his fate was sealed. Bizarrely, and despite a marked taste for violence, rape and murder, he is remembered as one of eighteenth-century London's most colourful and romantic characters.

James MacLaine – (executed 1750) and William Plunkett

With an accomplice called William Plunkett, vicar's son MacLaine robbed the aesthete and man of letters Horace Walpole while he was making his way home from Holland House across Hyde Park. Walpole was slightly injured by 'the pistol of one of them going off *accidentally*' (my italics), but after receiving a letter of apology from the highwayman later the same year he reported in his journal that 'my friend Mr M'Lean is hanged'.

John Rann – Executed 1774

Immortalised as 'Sixteen-String Jack' – a reference to coloured cords he wore attached to his knee breeches – John Rann was employed as a postilion and then a coachman. Something of a dandy, he turned to petty theft as his outgoings outgrew his income, and pickpocketing soon gave way to highway robbery. After holding up a member of the Royal Household at Brentford, an attendant on George II's daughter Princess Amelia, he found himself in Newgate Gaol. For his execution, he reportedly appeared in a pea-green suit with matching nosegay, and is commemorated today in the name of a pub in Theydon Bois at the eastern end of the Central Line.

FROM ROZZERS TO COPPERS – LONDON'S POLICE FORCE

Bantams

The nickname the City of London Police have for the men of the Met because the former used to have a 6-ft height restriction compared to just 5 ft 10 in. for the ordinary Old Bill.

Bill or Old Bill

This may be a nineteenth-century reference, when the cipher of William IV was embossed on police truncheons, although the police themselves make another dozen or so suggestions for the term's origins.

Bluebottle

Possibly a reference to the uniform, together with a piece of cockney rhyming slang, bottle being short for 'bottle and glass,' meaning arse.

Bobby

No longer widely used, but derived from the common diminutive of the name of the founder of the Force, Sir Robert Peel.

Boys in Blue

An obvious reference to the blue uniform worn by most officers.

Cop or Copper

Possibly an acronym for 'Constable on Patrol', but it has also been suggested that it refers to the metal bands on nineteenth-century truncheons.

Flatfoot

Now rarely used, but a reference to the fact that a beat bobby would traditionally have spent all day pounding the streets.

Fuzz

An American import from the 1960s.

Heat

See Fuzz.

Peeler

See Bobby.

Pig

Offensive and of surprisingly long standing, with possible nineteenth-century origins.

Plod

From Enid Blyton's village policeman, with female colleagues occasionally known as 'Plonks'.

Rozzers

'Rozzing' is an old East End term for roasting, although a French connection is also suggested from the continental criminal slang term '*roussin*' or '*rousse*', meaning redhead.

Sweeney

Specifically used to describe the Flying Squad, i.e. Sweeney Todd in rhyming slang.

Woodentops

Derived from the 1950s' children's BBC television series of this name but now rarely used.

London's Worst Ever Riots

1517 – Evil May Day

Following a call from the open-air pulpit of St Paul's Cross for 'Englishmen to cherish and defend themselves, and to hurt and grieve aliens for the common weal', Londoners ran riot through the streets of the City looking for foreign merchants and others whom they accused of deliberately ruining trade in London. Many were killed, and houses and business premises razed to the ground, before order was restored by militiamen under the command of two noblemen, the earls of Suffolk and Surrey. Hundreds of the rioters were arrested, but most were pardoned and, despite the death and carnage, a mere thirteen ringleaders were hanged, drawn and quartered.

1668 – The Bawdy House Riots

In seventeen-century London, Shrove Tuesday was traditionally celebrated by an invasion of brothels by young apprentices but, for reasons never made clear, things got out of hand in 1668. Various properties were smashed up in an apparent response to the perceived licentious behaviour of the newly restored Court, with Pepys referring to the chaos in his diary for 24 and 25 March. Nine offenders were subsequently sentenced to hang.

1780 – Gordon Riots

What started as a protest against the removal of certain anti-Catholic laws rapidly escalated as rabble-rousers attacked various foreign embassies and Roman chapels before moving on to public buildings such as Newgate Gaol and the Bank of England. Eventually, troops arrived to restore order, which they did by killing several hundred rioters, with more than two hundred wounded. More than twenty ringleaders were tried and executed but, incredibly, Lord George Gordon – the leader of the Protestant Association – was not among them.

1809 – The Old Price Riots

People frequently complain about the price of concert and West End theatre tickets, but when the latter were hiked from 3*s.* 6*d.* to 4*s.* to pay for a new Covent Garden Theatre (the old one had burned down in 1808) a portion of the population went berserk. The trouble started during a performance of *Macbeth*, with the arrival of Bow Street Runners only serving to fan the flames. Fortunately, the damage was not extensive, but for more than sixty days performances at the theatre were routinely disrupted and, eventually, the management backed down and ticket prices were restored to their pre-Fire levels.

1855 – Hyde Park Riots

When most working-class people had just one day off a week, a move to stop the buying and selling of goods on the Sabbath was enough for tens of thousands of 'artisans, mechanics, and lower orders of the metropolis' to gather in Hyde Park to protest. Before long, a witness reported 'mobs of boys and degraded women, under the guidance of stalwart ruffians or desperate Irishmen' parading the streets and levying contributions. Another observer – Karl Marx – excitedly predicted the coming of an English Revolution, but he was premature. The legislation to outlaw Sunday trading was quickly withdrawn, and the crowds soon melted away.

1886 – West End Riots

Essentially what started as left-wing protest about high rates of unemployment was allowed to get out of hand by an incompetently led police force that did nothing to prevent disgruntled gangs from making their way towards the shops of Piccadilly and the clubs of St James's. For allowing them to take their frustrations out on the upper classes in this way, the Met's Commissioner Sir Edmund Henderson was afterwards relieved of his post and a new Riot (Damages) Act was brought in enabling shop owners and others to claim compensation from the police.

1936 – Battle of Cable Street

The most famous protest of the Mosley era, the battle saw anti-fascists in pitched battles against squads of policemen who were determined to allow Sir Oswald's British Union of Fascists to march through a predominantly Jewish area of the East End. Protesters threw up barricades to prevent the reviled Blackshirts from passing down their streets, appalled that the Government would permit the march, and in the fighting around 175 were injured, including many women and children on the side of the protesters.

1958 – Notting Hill Riots

A violent response to the sudden rise in post-war immigration, rioting broke out in late August after a gang of white youths attacked a Scandinavian woman with a Jamaican husband. It was one of many such incidents that summer and, before long, hundreds of Teddy Boys and others were out on the streets attacking West Indians and their houses with petrol bombs. The police made more than 140 arrests, mostly of whites, and 9 youths received 'exemplary' sentences of 5 years. In a bid to build bridges, the inaugural Notting Hill Carnival was held the following year.

1990 – Poll Tax Riots

On the last day of March, a large gathering in Trafalgar Square, called to protest against the introduction of the Community Charge, exploded into senseless violence. A new 'Battle of Trafalgar' raged as thousands rampaged through the streets of the West End smashing up police cars and shops and looting property. Pubs were ordered to close, and wine bars in Covent Garden were set on fire. By the time the rioters were brought under control, more than 100 people had been injured, and 334 arrests had been made. The Community Charge was eventually replaced by a Council Tax, but feelings still run high in some quarters.

2011 – August Riots

For four days, hundreds – if not thousands – of looters smashed, broke and burned retail premises in response, it was said, to the shooting of a suspected armed man by police in Tottenham. As the contagion spread across the country, emergency 999 calls rose three-fold, all police leave was cancelled and, in London alone, nearly 3,500 individual crimes were linked to rioters. With 3,100 arrests and more than 1,000 people charged, courts were forced to sit for extended hours, their task made slightly easier by so many rioters smiling foolishly into security cameras as they looted their own neighbours' shops and homes.[1]

---

1 At more than 420,000, or nearly 1 per 20 people, London is now said to have the most CCTV cameras of any city in the world.

THE LAW REALLY IS AN ASS

When Peter the Great visited London he asked why there were so many lawyers. 'I have but two in my whole dominion,' he is reported to have said. 'And I believe I shall hang one of them when I get home.'

Part of the reason for the number, of course, could be to cope with all the laws we have – so many of which have never made sense to the majority.

Freemen of the City of London, for example, are still entitled to **drive sheep** across London's bridges – this has been tested recently, and proved – as well as to carry a sword within the historic square mile and, should they choose to do so, to accompany a gaggle of geese along Cheapside.

Until the 1960s, **nude women** were permitted on the London stage but only providing they remained completely still. The government official responsible for ensuring the law was observed in this way was called Sir George Titman.

Despite the popular cockney ballad, the Metropolitan Police Act (1839) means Londoners may not **roll out the barrel** if this means rolling it down a pavement.

Golf can be played on Wimbledon Common but only by individuals wearing a **red outer garment**.

Incredibly, it is also an offence to possess a **pack of cards** if staying 'within a mile of any arsenal or explosives store'.

Under the terms of section 60 (3) of the Metropolitan Police Act (1829), Londoners may not **beat a carpet** on the street after 8.00 a.m.

Section 54 of the same Act outlaws the **flying of kites** in any street or thoroughfare where to do so might risk annoying somebody else, and makes it an offence to carry a plank along the pavement. (The Act allows for a penalty of up to £1,000 or fourteen days in prison for anyone who does so.)

Shoppers in Burlington Arcade on Piccadilly are not allowed to **run, sing or whistle** or to open an umbrella – although one of the uniformed beadles once informed Sir Paul McCartney that as a former Beatle he is exempt from this restriction.

A law dating back to 1279 means Members of Parliament may not attend the House of Commons wearing a **suit of armour**, nor, it is popularly supposed, may they die on the premises. (As the Palace of Westminster is technically a Royal Palace it is thought this might entitle the deceased to a State Funeral, but this has been questioned as Guy Fawkes, Sir Walter Raleigh and Spencer Perceval were not afforded a State funeral, and they were all killed there.)

Any **sturgeon or whale** recovered from the Thames automatically belongs to the monarch.

City of London butchers are theoretically still liable to spend a day in the pillory if they knowingly **sell bad meat**.

Women are now permitted to **eat chocolate** on the Underground following the repeal of an idiotic late nineteenth-century regulation.

Venal Vicars and Conniving Con Men

Vicar – John Wilkinson

Hoping to profit from the unique status of the Queen's Chapel of the Savoy – situated off the Strand, it is literally the Queen's chapel, a personal possession of the monarch rather than of the London Diocese – in 1754, Wilkinson conceived a plan to celebrate marriages here that would otherwise be illegal. For two years, he got away with it, with as many as 1,400 sham 'Savoy Marriages' being conducted (many of them after dark) before he was arrested. Tried on the basis that he did 'unlawfully, knowingly, wilfully and feloniously solemnise' marriages, and found guilty, he was transported for fourteen years.

Con Man – Michael Corrigan

In post-war London, Michael Corrigan was the epitome of an impeccably turned-out major in the Brigade of Guards, with a solid war record and a suitably clipped, cut-glass accent. Unfortunately, it was all bogus, but his cheek and charm enabled him to sell the Tower of London to a stranger, London Bridge at least twice, and a Piccadilly mansion to a credulous American tourist. He was arrested after trying to offload something else on to the Director of Public Prosecutions – in the bar of the Ritz, of course – and, after being convicted of fraud, he hanged himself using an old regimental tie.

Vicar – William Dodd

The son of a vicar and one himself, Dr Dodd was a bright but impecunious Cambridge scholar who married before he could afford to, squandered a handsome lottery win, and was eventually executed after resorting to bribery and forgery to fund his lifestyle. In 1774, in an attempt to win a lucrative position, Dodd had attempted to bribe the Lord Chancellor's wife, and, when that failed, produced a fake cheque for £4,200 drawn on a friend's account. For such an enormous sum, he was sentenced to hang, and did so despite a 23,000-name petition appealing for clemency.

Con Man – Charles Tyson Yerkes

A former jailbird who played a major role in developing the London Underground, Yerkes was a canny American operator whose rule of business was simply to 'buy up old junk, fix it up a little and unload it upon other fellows'. When that failed, he would happily resort to bribery and blackmail. In London, he masqueraded as a multi-millionaire to secure control over the Metropolitan, District, Bakerloo, Piccadilly and Northern Lines, but when he died in 1905 he was effectively penniless, and a fire sale was needed to clear his massive debts.

Vicar – Harold Davidson

Defrocked in 1932 for engaging in a licentious lifestyle, the celebrated Rector of Stiffkey was a comedy mime artist before taking his vows. He acquired the soubriquet of 'the Prostitute's Padre' after being discovered consorting with the ladies of Soho when he should have been ministering to his Norfolk flock. Assured of a measure of celebrity by the case's juicy details, but deprived of his living, Davidson left Soho and set off around England to work once more as an entertainer. While posing as 'Daniel in the Lion's Den' to amuse the folk of Skegness, he was unfortunately mauled by the usually placid Freddie and died of his wounds.

Con Man – Lord Gordon-Gordon

Conning a London jeweller out of £25,000 and US railwayman Jay Gould out of an incredible $1 million in 1873, Gordon-Gordon was caught and arrested but jumped bail and fled to Canada. Frustrated in their attempts to extradite him back to the USA, five of his dupes – including two future State Governors, and three future Congressmen – attempted to kidnap him and themselves ended up in gaol. Gordon-Gordon threw a massive party to celebrate his freedom, before shooting himself in the head. More than a century later, it's still not certain who he was.

Vicar – Edmund Bonner

Nicknamed 'Bloody Bonner' and widely reviled, the sixteenth-century Bishop of London became notorious for his role in the persecution and execution of supposed heretics during the Catholic rule of Mary I of England. During her short reign, and with Bonner presiding, around 300 Protestants were burned at the stake.

When Mary died in 1558, her sister's accession to the throne sealed Bonner's fate. Confined to the Tower on Elizabeth's orders, he attempted to convert his fellow prisoners before being moved to the Marshalsea Gaol where he later died. He was buried at night and in secret to avoid inflaming public anger.

Con Man – Robert Hendy-Freegard

A former barman and London car salesman who for years posed as an MI5 agent, Hendy-Freegard was jailed in 2005 after fleecing his lovers of hundreds of thousands of pounds. He did this by drawing them into an imaginary world of espionage, Mafia and IRA death threats. Warning them not to speak to anyone else, isolating his victims was a masterstroke, but, unfortunately for Hendy-Freegard, the FBI took an interest when he chanced upon an American. Following an elaborate sting operation at Heathrow Airport, he was charged with kidnapping and found guilty of eighteen counts of theft and deception.

18

Sporting London

'I was always a sports nut but I've lost interest now in whether one bunch of mercenaries in North London is going to beat another bunch of mercenaries from West London.'

John Cleese

Never mind the annual Tweed Run, London's strangest cycle race took place in 1993 some 130 ft below ground level. It ran through the 50-mile-long Thames Water Ring Main (see Chapter 5) before this was filled with water.

Hard to believe but, prior to losing 6–3 to Hungary at Wembley in November 1953, England had never lost a football match to a team from outside the UK.

The West End street known as Pall Mall takes its name from '*paille-maille*', a seventeenth-century precursor to croquet that was played here.

Hippodrome Place in Notting Hill marks the site of a race track where horses competed until 1842.

Until it was destroyed in the Blitz, the most popular boxing arena in London was the former Surrey Chapel near Blackfriar's Bridge.

Since 1959, the Great Tube Challenge has seen crazy commuters racing to visit all 269 stations on the Underground as quickly as possible. The present record stands at just over 18.5 hours, and is proving incredibly hard to beat.

The first ever FA Cup Final took place not at Wembley but at the Kennington Oval. In 1872, the Wanderers beat the Royal Engineers 1–0.

London may not have got its first ice-skating rink until the 1840s (see Chapter 13), but the Museum of London has a pair of ice-skates that are much, much older. Fitted with bone blades, these are thought to date back to the twelfth century.

The name of Penny Brookes Street in Stratford commemorates Dr William Penny Brookes, a nineteenth-century medic who campaigned to get PE put on the curriculum in schools. He also invited Baron de Coubertin to witness his local Much Wenlock Games in Shropshire, after which the Frenchman went on to launch the modern Olympic movement.

Although the Olympic Games didn't come to London until 1908 (see panel below), the city played a key role in establishing the first Athens Games in 1896. Enthusiastic but inexperienced, the Greeks had no understanding of track building – not for the previous 1,500 years anyway – and so borrowed a groundsman from Stamford Bridge, Mr Charles Perry, to supervise the work.

London 1908 – Olympic Highlights

British archers **William and Charlotte Dod** became the first ever brother and sister Olympic medallists. Away from White City, the extraordinarily versatile Charlotte also won the British Ladies Amateur Golf Championship – and Wimbledon, five times.

Winning the Running Deer Shooting Single Shot event, **Oscar Swahn**, aged 60, became the oldest ever competitor to earn an Olympic gold medal, and then the next day did it again.

Sweden's **Frithiof Martensson** sportingly agreed to postpone the Middleweight Greco-Roman Wrestling final to allow his rival to recover from a slight injury – and was rewarded with a gold medal when he won the bout.

In the marathon, the first man into the stadium, Italy's **Dorando Pietri**, took a wrong turn and then collapsed. He was disqualified after being helped to his feet by officials but afterwards received a special trophy from Queen Alexandra who felt genuinely sorry for him.

Britain took all the medals in **racquets** and **tug of war** after entering multiple teams for events no other country had even heard of, and assured itself of victory in the **rowing** by banning competitors who had previously rowed the Thames unless they were British.

The home team was also assisted ever so slightly by Britain's insistence that it would supply all the **officials** needed to run, monitor, rule and judge every event throughout the

Games. Without any outside scrutiny or interference, one British competitor was even awarded a winning decision by his own father.

Also slightly suspect was the newly introduced Olympic sport of **motor boating**, which saw the fabulously rich Duke of Westminster competing against the only-slightly-less-so Baron Howard de Walden. Curiously enough, the sport was dropped from the Games immediately afterwards.

For the Games to be run here in 1908, a new 'Great Stadium' was needed, and one was built at White City in just ten months at a cost of only £60,000. With seating for 68,000 spectators and twice that number standing, it was the world's biggest and, over the coming decades, was to host everything from athletics and greyhound racing to speedway and even a round of the 1966 World Cup. It was torn down in 1985, and the giant Westfield shopping centre now covers much of the site.

The odd length of the modern marathon at 26 miles and 385 yards is a purely London creation. Before 1908, the event was run over 25 miles, but the decision was taken to increase this so that the race could start beneath the windows of the Royal Nursery at Windsor Castle (for the pleasure of the young Royals) and finish opposite the Royal Box in the stadium.

When the Games returned to London in 1948, the decision was taken to bar Germany and Japan. Oddly, the Italians were still invited, however, despite having been on the losing side in the war and, indeed, having been the pioneers of fascism ever since embracing Benito Mussolini.

London 1948 – Olympic Highlights

The star of the Games, **Fanny Blankers-Koen**, equalled black athlete Jesse Owens' historic medal tally at Adolf Hitler's 1936 Berlin Olympics but could conceivably have done even better. Unfortunately, the Olympics at this time had a rule limiting women, as the weaker sex, to three individual events in track and field events.

Having had his right hand damaged by an exploding grenade a decade earlier, the Hungarian shooter **Karoly Takacs** taught himself to shoot with his left hand and won an Olympic gold medal in the Rapid-Fire Pistol event.

Arthur Wint became the first of many Jamaicans to strike Olympic gold (in the Men's 400 m) while high-jumper **Alice Coachman** became the first African-American woman to win a gold medal in a track-and-field event.

In **Diving**, all four gold medals, and six out of the remaining eight silver and bronze medals, were won by the USA. **Victoria Manalo Draves** won both golds in the women's events, with **Sammy Lee** winning a gold and a bronze in the men's.

Uniquely, a three-way tie was declared for the men's **Pommel Horse**, with all three Finnish gymnasts each being awarded a gold medal with no silver or bronze being presented.

Refusing to return home with the athletes following her county's inclusion in the Soviet Bloc, Czechoslovakia team president **Marie Provaznikova** became the first defector in Olympic history.

A notable member of the American team, Hawaii-born **Toshiyuki 'Harold' Sakata**, won weightlifting silver and went on to play the part of Oddjob in the 007 film, *Goldfinger*.

The Games were also the first to introduce some important **technological innovations**, including starting blocks for runners and what became known as the photo finish.

In post-war, 'austerity' Britain there were no resources to build an athletes' village so, for 1948, competitors were billeted in some of London's many disused military barracks. They were shipped into the arena using army trucks, with British athletes expected to stay at home or make their own arrangements.

Ahead of the Games, in an early exercise in recycling, many tons of waste from household fires in Leicester were collected and brought to London to build a new cinder track at Wembley.

Few records were broken this time round, however, perhaps because the competitors were too hungry to give their best. With rationing still in force, consideration had been given to asking the teams to bring their own food, but eventually the rules were waived and competitors were allowed 5,500 calories a day – compared to 2,600 for ordinary Londoners.

1948 also saw the BBC's first foray into large-scale sports coverage, the Corporation paying a hefty £1,000 for the rights to televise the Games. Viewers were promised sixty-four hours of action from the various sports fields, although hardly anyone could actually afford to own a television set at this time.

As in 2012, the events were widely spread across London, with boxing, wrestling and gymnastics taking place in West Kensington (on a site now covered by the Empress State Building), and cyclists being trucked out to the Victorian velodrome that still survives in Herne Hill.

LONDON 2012 – BORIS JOHNSON'S GOLDEN MOMENTS

'The excitement is growing so much I think the Geiger counter of Olympo-mania is going to go "zoink" off the scale.'

'Get some burgers, or else you'll be eaten by bears . . .' (on hearing that McDonald's was to sponsor the supposed fitness-fest).

'The whole of the exterior of this building [the Velodrome] *is lovingly rubbed with rhubarb.'*

'I had hot tears of patriotic pride from the beginning [of the opening ceremony]. *I was blubbing like Andy Murray.'*

'It is hard to think of a single Chinese sport at the Olympics, compared with umpteen invented by Britain, including ping-pong, I'll have you know, which originated at upper-class dinner tables and was first called whiff-whaff.'

'There are semi-naked women playing beach volleyball in the middle of the Horse Guards Parade immortalised by Canaletto. They are glistening like wet otters and the water is splashing off the brims of the spectators' sou'westers.'

'The whole thing is magnificent and bonkers.'

'"Inspire a generation" is our motto. Not necessarily "Create a generation" . . . which is what they sometimes get up to in the Olympic village.'

'In the heart of the Olympic Park, there are riparian meadows of wildflowers whose colour and glory are heart-breaking. There are cornflowers and viper's bugloss and rare and delicate orchids that are being neither trampled nor picked – but simply admired, by vast crowds, as evidence of our national genius for gardening.'

'I think we are showing great natural restraint and politeness as host nation in not hoarding the medals more so far.'

19

Driving London

'London Transport commissioned a study to find out why buses were running late and it turned out it was because they kept stopping to let people on.'

Rory McGrath

London's Famous Motoring Firsts

One of several significant London motoring firsts, the traffic island was the idea of a Colonel Pierpoint who came up with it in the 1860s. Placing the first at the top of St James's Street, one assumes so that he could cross safely to his club, the Colonel was naturally proud of his creation and was in the habit of turning round to admire it. Unfortunately, on one occasion he missed his footing as he did so and was promptly run over by a cab.

In those days, of course, his nemesis arrived with a horse up front as the first mechanically driven versions didn't make their appearance until 1897. But even when they did, and despite their very considerable novelty value at the time, these early pioneers were considerably slower than their horse-drawn alternatives and the fashion for them was soon exhausted.

As a result, having led the world with this new technology in the closing days of the Victorian era, by the start of the Edwardian era there were still only nineteen automobiles trundling around central London – compared to 10,361 conventional horse-drawn vehicles on London's streets, the last of which survived until just after the Second World War (see Taxi! panel below).

London's first set of traffic lights appeared at the junction of Great George Street and Bridge Street in 1868. Designed by Superintendent John Peake Knight of the South-Eastern Railway, it used semaphore arms as well as lights but was gas-powered and unfortunately blew up, killing a policeman and causing a cavalry stampede. The semaphore arms were intended to replicate a policeman's arms, but the experiment was abandoned and London remained light-free until 1929.

The first ever multi-storey car park made a surprisingly early debut, too, opening for business in 1901 when motorcars were still an expensive rarity. Located immediately behind Piccadilly Circus in Denman Street (where today NCP still offers a similar, if somewhat costlier, service), it covered more than 19,000 sq ft on no fewer than seven storeys. The upper ones were reached via a hydraulic lift rather than a ramp, a device capable of raising a three-ton vehicle. If nothing else, the existence of such a facility so early on suggests that almost a century ago parking in central London was already quite a considerable problem.

This then begs the question: why did it take so long to introduce the parking meter? First seen sprouting out of the sidewalks of Oklahoma City in the USA, it wasn't until 1958 that British motorists got some of their own. Once again, London led the way, with a handful appearing on the pavements of Mayfair at a time when 1*s.* (5p) would be sufficient to keep the authorities at bay for a full hour.

London can lay claim to Britain's first successful self-service petrol station, too, and this country's first-ever drive-in bank. Designed with passing motorists in mind, the latter was installed by the venerable Drummond's Bank (now part of the Royal Bank of Scotland) in a building by Admiralty Arch on Trafalgar Square. London also got the country's first traffic police. While lacking vehicles of their own, the earliest recruits were issued with so-called 'egg bombs' – filled with green and white paint – to hurl at any speeding motorists.

TAXI!

Sadly, looking like it's about to be consigned to a museum, London's iconic black cab has a surprisingly ancient heritage. The now defunct Corporation of Coachmen first secured a charter to ply for hire in London in 1639, the word 'cab' being derived from the French, '*cabriolet de place*'.

Despite being licensed by Parliament, cabs at first failed to attract the right class of customer, and in 1694 a group of women travelling in one through Hyde Park behaved so badly that cab drivers were henceforth banned from royal parks for the next 230 years.

Cabbies had a reputation for getting drunk and behaving badly until a number of Victorian philanthropists paid for distinctive dark-green cab shelters to be built where drivers could stop for lunch. Drinking alcohol in them was forbidden, together with any talk of politics and, of the original sixty-four, around a dozen still survive.

London's first mechanically driven taxis appeared in the 1890s but were electric rather than petrol-powered. Their novelty value was enormous but, unfortunately, they were so heavy – all those batteries – that the horse-drawn competition was quicker. It took nearly sixty years for motorised taxis finally to rule the road.

The official name of a black cab is a Hackney Carriage, but this has no connection with the East London suburb. Instead, it comes from an old French term, '*haquenée*', meaning an ambling old nag or horse.

Horse-drawn cabs survived until the 1940s, largely because of police reluctance to license any kind of new technology. Gottlieb Daimler invented the internal combustion engine in 1883, and built a petrol-powered cab soon afterwards, but it was more than two decades before the Metropolitan Police agreed to allow such a newfangled contraption on to the streets.

The taximeter was invented in 1891 by Wilhelm Bruhn, and gives the cab its familiar name. Introduced to London in 1907, it indicated the distance travelled in order to prevent rows with the driver about the size of the fare.

In France, taxis were used to take troops to the front in the First World War, but back in London their numbers slumped by more than half when petrol shortages gave the horse another brief advantage.

Long after horse-drawn cabs were gone for good, London cabbies were still governed by a number of weird rules and regulations dating back centuries. For decades, cabs had to be designed with a space next to the driver for a bale of hay, and with sufficient headroom in the back to accommodate a man in a top hat, but this rule was finally abolished in 1976.

Some of the archaic laws concerning cabs do still exist, however, and can affect passengers as well. We're not meant to shout 'Taxi!' at a moving vehicle, for example – it's technically a breach of the law – but instead to go to a taxi rank, or what the rules quaintly define as 'a place appointed'.

Perhaps the most bizarre of the regulations relating to cabbies in London is a law requiring drivers to answer the call of nature 'against the rear of the vehicle, and in a seemly fashion'. In theory, any taxi driver embarrassed about doing this can ask a police constable to shield them with his cape.

Taxi drivers are also forbidden to carry passengers who admit to having a notifiable disease such as bubonic plague or smallpox, and can refuse to pick up anyone they suspect of harbouring such a disease.

Drivers also have to avoid driving too slowly. If they do, they can be charged with loitering – or with 'driving too furiously' if they are caught speeding within London's historic Square Mile.

Although modern black cabs look pretty similar, the classic London black cab was the old Austin FX4, which was introduced in 1958 and remained in production until 1996. That's a record for a British vehicle, one that is unrivalled by any make except the original Mini, and that is unlikely to be beaten by any of its replacements.

For a while, London black cabs went on sale in the Far East, where they were badged as 'Big Ben Novelty Cars', but the most famous version was a luxury model of the FX4 built for the oil billionaire Nubar Gulbenkian. 'Apparently, it can turn on a sixpence . . .' he used to tell his friends. '. . . whatever that is.' (The Duke of Edinburgh had a smarter-than-average one for a while, too, liveried in British Racing Green on the outside, and tan leather within.)

In 1885, a man called John Leighton wrote to the GPO suggesting the boundaries of London be redrawn to make each individual borough a regular hexagon two miles across. This, he said, would enable travellers to consult a map and see at once how much their journey would cost by cab, but fortunately the introduction of the taximeter rendered his scheme redundant.

Roadside petrol pumps, of course, were in themselves nothing new, and the first in this country appeared in Shropshire before the First World War. But self-service stations were decidedly novel, the first practical one opening for business in London in November 1961 at the foot of Southwark Bridge. (The idea had been tried before, at Patcham in Sussex in the 1930s, but unfortunately it relied on a primitive 'shilling-in-the-slot' pump and the honesty of the locals – neither of which proved to be at all dependable.)

It was in London, too, that the first dedicated club for automobilists opened, the lavishly appointed Royal Automobile Club at 89 Pall Mall. Its nickname was and is the Chauffeur's Arms, a sneering reference to its relative youth – the clubhouse was only completed in 1911 – and the fact that it is by far the least exclusive of the traditional St James's gentlemen's clubs. That said, with its Turkish baths, squash doubles court, a private post office and what is still the capital's most beautiful swimming pool, its facilities are the best of any West End club – and the neighbours know it.

Occupying the site of the old War Office – parts of which were incorporated into the clubhouse – it was designed by Charles Mewes and Arthur J. Davis, architects of the Ritz Hotel. The building was hugely advanced for its day, too – those early motorists were naturally more technically minded than most – with an eight-storey, 2,000-ton steel skeleton supporting the immense Portland stone façade. This behemoth's arrival on such a prominent site was not universally welcomed in clubland, however; members of older and socially much smarter establishments clearly deplored what one of their number described as a 'furred, goggled, spare-tyred and cigar-smoking crowd'.

As to the reason for all this, the car itself, London cannot claim to have built the first but it has certainly been responsible for some pretty odd examples. Willesden was home to the Iris factory, from 1905 until the outbreak of the Great War, churning out a cumbersome and rather crudely made tourer named for the goddess of the same name. She was known as the Speedy Messenger of the Gods, although the name was also said by the factory to indicate (somewhat optimistically) that 'It Runs In Silence'.

Then there was E. H. Owen of Kensington, a shadowy outfit that, from 1899 until 1935, advertised in *The Autocar* and elsewhere. It claimed to be a car manufacturer, but no such car as an 'Owen' was ever seen and nor has the precise location of the factory ever been discovered.

And finally, a major player still with us today and one that was first established just over the river in Lambeth. The original factory took its name from the home of a medieval warrior who once lived on the site on the south bank of the Thames, and when the company relocated to Luton – coincidentally where the warrior had had his country seat – it took his heraldic emblem to use on the company badge. The warrior was called Fulk le Bréant, his home was Fulk's or Fawke's Hall, and the warrior's griffin is still to be found on the front of every car which leaves the Vauxhall factory.

Motoring's Most Distinctive Extinctions

Bridget Driscoll

At Crystal Palace in 1896, Bridget made her mark in history as the first person to be killed by a car. The car was moving at just 4 mph, and today the running total of motoring fatalities is thought to exceed 30 million worldwide. (The first driver to die was Edwin Sewell three years later. He was thrown from his 6 hp Daimler in Grove Hill, Harrow, when a rear wheel collapsed, and his passenger died shortly afterwards in hospital.)

Graham Hill

Born in Hampstead in 1929, Graham Hill is still the only driver to win motorsport's Triple Crown, meaning the Formula One

World Championship, the Le Mans 24-Hour Race and America's Indianapolis 500. Unfortunately, he lost when he took part in the BBC's *Call My Bluff* and, in 1979, died after crashing his plane while trying to land in thick fog north of London.

Eleanor Thornton

A Stockwell girl, and almost certainly the model for Rolls-Royce's celebrated flying lady bonnet mascot, the Spirit of Ecstasy. Thornton was lost at sea in 1915 when the SS *Persia* went down after being torpedoed by a German U-boat. Her lover survived, Lord Montagu of Beaulieu having taken the precaution of donning a life-vest before losing hold of his mistress.

Cecil Kimber

Fired from his own company and working as a travelling salesman, MG founder Cecil Kimber died in a 1945 train derailment outside King's Cross. Bizarrely, the only other fatality had the same first name and initials – Cecil Kirk. Kimber himself had only been on the train because he had no petrol coupons left to fill up his MG.

Percy Lambert

Percy Lambert, the first motorist ever to travel 100 miles in one hour, was killed at the Brooklands circuit while trying to beat his own record. He was buried at London's fashionable Brompton Cemetery in 1913 (see Chapter 7), and interred in a coffin stylishly streamlined to match the Talbot car in which he died.

Rudolf Diesel

Last seen alive in September 1913, the pioneering engineer

drowned on his way to London on the steamer *Dresden*. Theories suggesting both murder and suicide have been advanced, but it took ten days to find his body, by which time it was so badly decomposed that a postmortem was no longer possible.

Eric Fernihough

The last Englishman ever to hold the World Land Speed Record for motorcycle and sidecar, a feat he accomplished riding that most English of marques – the Brough Superior – at Gyon in Hungary. It's somewhat appropriate, then – if a little premature – that the thirty-three-year-old Fernihough died on St George's Day 1938 shortly after his new and improved Brough had been unveiled at London's Earl's Court.

Hon. Charles Stewart Rolls

A younger son of Lord Llangattock, the co-founder of the eponymous car company was a fearless balloonist and a ferociously quick driver but, in 1910, died when the tail of his Wright Flyer became detached. The first Briton to be killed in a flying accident, he was only the eleventh air fatality worldwide and is commemorated by a blue plaque at 14 Conduit Street, Mayfair, which was his place of work from 1905 to 1910.

London's Fastest Ladies

Hon. Mrs Victor Bruce

The first woman ever prosecuted for speeding (she told Hounslow magistrates driving slowly made her tired), in 1929 Mrs Bruce drove a 4.5-litre Bentley at Montlhéry for twenty-four hours, capturing the world record for single-handed driving at an average of 89 mph.

Flying round the world solo the following year, she famously switched off her engine over Hong Kong, China to observe two minutes' silence for Armistice Day.

Lady Mary Grosvenor

A favourite daughter of Bend'Or, the fabulously rich 2nd Duke of Westminster, Lady Mary died in 2003 aged 89. Before the war, she raced regularly at Brooklands, favouring a 1.5-litre Alta over Bugattis but denying herself a 2.0-litre Grand Prix version, perhaps because her father disapproved.

Violet Cordery

Described in the *Daily Telegraph* as 'the Amy Johnson of the track', in July 1927 Cordery arrived back in London having become the first woman to circumnavigate the globe by car. She did so in an Invicta, designed by her brother-in-law Sir Noel Macklin.

Roberta Cowell

A student at University College London, in the 1940s Robert Cowell flew Spitfires but then, in 1951, changed his name to Roberta after undergoing Britain's first ever sex-change operation.

Dorothy Levitt

In 1906, Hackney-born Levitt lifted the women's world speed record to 96 mph. The same year her book *The Woman and the Car* advised readers to carry a hand mirror in their toolkits, which she said was useful to 'restore a gel's complexion' after a drive and could also be held aloft to check behind while driving in heavy traffic.

Barbara Cartland

Originally a Midlands lass but always giving an impression of being more at home in Belgravia than Birmingham, the romantic authoress and fluffy pink socialite organised the first ever ladies' race at Brooklands (in 1931) and claimed to have invented the concept of the troop-carrying glider.

WHY ARE LONDON BUSES RED?

In 1907, the year that route numbers were introduced across London, there was very fierce competition for passengers among the capital's many small, independent bus companies. As private firms, they were free to paint their vehicles any colour they chose, and the largest of them – the London General Omnibus Company – decided to make its buses stand out from those of its rivals by adopting bright red paint and a new logo. For the latter, LGOC chose a spoked wheel design, a feature that eventually evolved into the world-famous London Transport (and subsequently Transport for London) 'roundel'.

By the time the ongoing process of consolidation and nationalisation had led to the creation of the new London Transport organisation in 1933, red was the predominant colour for buses in the capital and it has remained so ever since. Today, there are 8,500 of them in service covering approximately 700 routes and calling at more than 19,500 bus stops along the way. With more than 2 billion passenger trips made annually, it is estimated that 90 per cent of Londoners live within 400 yards of a bus stop.

London Cabbie Slang

'Arnie' – 'I'll be back', meaning the driver is not yet going home.

'B&B' – a routine check by the police (i.e. of a driver's green badge and his licence, known as a bill).

'Bilker' – a customer the driver expects to do a runner without paying.

'Blue Lights' – police dealing with an incident.

'Blue Trees' – a policeman hiding behind a tree or lamppost with a speed gun.

'Broom' – a job the driver passes on to the next in the rank as he doesn't want it.

'Butterboy' – a novice cabbie.

'Butterfly' – part-time cabbie, only works in nice weather.

'Canary' – a driver with a yellow badge, meaning he can only work in the suburbs.

'Carpet' – £3, i.e. three feet to the yard.

'Ching' – £5.

'Churchill' – a meal; Winston Churchill is said to have given drivers the right to refuse a fare if they're eating.

'Cooking' – spending too long on a rank without a fare.

'Droshky' – a taxi.

'Full House' – full complement of passengers.

'Gavroched' – when the traffic in Mayfair is so bad the driver could get out and read the menu at this much-starred Upper Brook Street restaurant.

'Hickory' – hickory-dickory dock (i.e. clock, meaning the meter).

'Kojak with a Kodak' – see Blue Trees (above).

'Legalled' – receiving the correct fare but no tip.

'Mexican wave' – a pavement full of potential fares holding up their hands.

'Oner' – a long job, paying £100.

'ONO' – On and off (i.e. arriving at a rank and pulling straight off with a punter).

'Penguin' – passenger going to or being collected from a formal event.

'Scab' – minicab.

'Set' – an accident.

'Sherb' – sherbert dab, taxicab.

'Single pin' – solo passenger.

'Stalking' – working with the meter off.

'Suit' – city gent.

'Turkish' – a laugh (short for Turkish bath).

Parliamentarian Wisdom on Motoring in London

'I do not believe the introduction of motor cars will ever affect the riding of horses.'

John Scott Montagu MP (1903)

'Depend upon it, if these motorists and motor cars are not kept in order they will have to leave the roads altogether because in the long run the people will never submit to the intolerable nuisance which has been created.'

C. A. Cripps MP (1903)

'I do not think it would be practicable to introduce traffic islands in London.'

Wilfred Ashley MP, Minister of Transport (1928)

'We are satisfied that driving tests have absolutely no value.'

Lord Russell, Government Spokesman on Roads (1929)

'We must make the motorist feel that when he is discourteous and inconsiderate on the road he is not a British gentleman.'

Herbert Morrison MP, Minister for Transport (1930)

'My own view is that we shall have to ration cars. We shall have to have a waiting list.'

James Lovat-Fraser (1935), on the news that there were around 220,000 cars on Britain's roads. Today, the figure is more than 30 million.

20

Parliamentary London

'The problem is that many MPs never see the London that exists beyond the wine bars and brothels of Westminster.'

Ken Livingstone

Ten Peculiarities of the 'Mother of Parliaments'

Britain has the oldest parliament in the world but is one of only a handful of countries with no written constitution. (Israel, New Zealand and San Marino don't have one either.)

Despite an unusually long history of democracy, this country still requires the Queen to give her permission – or Royal Assent – for an Act of Parliament to pass into law. Fortunately, no monarch has refused to grant this permission since 1708.

Although the Queen takes care not to interfere with parliamentary procedure, no session is allowed to take place without the gold Mace – a symbol of her authority – being present in the chamber.

Bizarrely, the apportioning of parliamentary seats bears little relation to the number of votes cast. In 2005, Labour polled only 37 per cent of the vote but got well in excess of half the seats.

British voters have no say in who gets to be Prime Minister. Once a general election has been won, the leader of the party with the most seats – not votes – goes to Buckingham Palace to ask the Queen for permission to form a Government. Between elections, the governing party can also decide independently to switch leaders, as Labour did from Blair to Brown.

If no party wins an overall majority, it is quite possible for the least popular parties to get together to form a Government and, in theory, for a party to come last and still end up with its leader in No. 10.

There is no fixed period between one election and the next, although the law states that no more than five years must pass before a new election is called. This enables the party in power to choose the date that best suits them, an inherent form of bias.

The House of Lords exists in law to moderate the actions of the House of Commons, although the Parliament Acts of 1911 and 1949 mean their lordships – who these days are anyway mostly political appointees – can be ignored if they cause too much trouble.

Despite unruly behaviour and a lot of bad-tempered banter, MPs are still forbidden from swearing or from offering personal insults such as calling a member on the opposite benches a liar, coward, hooligan, traitor, guttersnipe or git. (Once, after being censured for calling half the cabinet 'asses', Benjamin Disraeli turned to the Speaker and, by way of an apology, declared, 'I withdraw. Half the Cabinet are not asses.')

Parliamentary Firsts

The first woman to take her seat in the House of Commons was **Nancy Astor** (1879–1964). An American who took on her husband's Plymouth seat when he succeeded to a viscountcy and moved to the House of Lords, Lady Astor entered the Commons in 1919.

The first woman to be elected to the lower house, however, was **Constance Markievicz** (1868–1927) a year earlier. The London-born daughter of the polar explorer Sir Henry Gore-Booth, as a member for Sinn Féin she chose to abide by the Irish party's abstentionist policy and did not enter the House. The same year, she was imprisoned in Holloway for campaigning against conscription.

In 1847, **Baron Lionel de Rothschild** similarly became the first Jewish Member of Parliament in this country. However, he refused to swear the oath of office as it included the phrase 'on the true faith of a Christian' and so was deemed unable to take his seat in the Commons. He stood down but was elected again three years later when, once again, he was denied the chance to sit when he refused to take the oath in its existing form.

Fortunately the law – and the oath – was finally changed in 1858, enabling **Sir David Salomons, Bt.** (1797–1873) to take his seat and become the first Jew ever to speak in the House. He was also the first Jewish Lord Mayor of London.

Britain's first Asian MP was **Dadabhai Naoroji** (1825–1917), a Professor of Mathematics and Natural Philosophy in Bombay and later of Gujarati at University College London. He was elected in the Liberal interest for Finsbury Central at the 1892 General Election.

Incredibly, it was to take nearly a hundred years for any Afro-Caribbeans to be elected, but in 1987 **Bernie Grant, Diane Abbott** and **Paul Boateng** secured three London constituencies for Labour. Of these, the last-named, now Lord Boateng of Aykem and Wembley, became the first ever black Cabinet minister in May 2002.

At 5.15 p.m. on 11 May 1812, **Spencer Perceval** became the first British Prime Minister to be murdered, and also the first MP to die within the Palace of Westminster. He was shot dead by a disgruntled voter, John Bellingham, leaving behind a widow and twelve children and just over £100 in the bank. Incredibly, 185 years later, descendants of Perceval and Bellingham stood against each other in the 1997 election, but neither man won.

Henry Fawcett (1833–84) was Britain's first blind MP; **Jack Ashley** (1922–2012) was the first to be totally deaf; and **Major Sir Jack Cohen** (1886–1965) was the first disabled MP. Having lost both legs at Ypres during the Great War, Sir Jack was elected to represent the Conservatives at Liverpool Fairfield in 1918 and held the seat for more than a dozen years.

DISHONOURABLE MEMBERS (I)

POLITICIAN LAW-BREAKERS

John Aislabie

Heavily implicated in the famous South Sea Bubble scandal in March 1721, Aislabie was found guilty of 'the most notorious, dangerous and infamous corruption' and, following his resignation from the Exchequer, he was expelled from the House of Commons and locked up in the Tower.

Jonathan Aitken

After launching an ill-advised libel case against the *Guardian* newspaper and Granada TV's *World in Action* in 1997, Conservative MP Aitken was subsequently charged with perjury and found guilty of perverting the course of justice. Jailed for eighteen months, he undertook a course in theology, and, 'born again', is now president of Christian Solidarity Worldwide.

Chris Huhne

In 2012, a simple speeding offence ballooned into a far more serious charge of perverting the course of justice when the Liberal Democrat Secretary of State admitted arranging for his wife to collect three penalty points, which were correctly due to him after a high-speed run down the M11 nearly a decade earlier. While awaiting sentencing, Huhne ensured his place in history by becoming only the fifth Privy Counsellor to resign in more than 500 years.

John Stonehouse

Faking his own death in 1974 – by leaving a pile of clothes on a Miami beach – the Labour MP was shortly afterwards arrested in Australia by officers who thought they had collared Lord Lucan. Charged with twenty-one counts of fraud, theft, forgery and wasting police time, his trial took sixty-eight days, after which he was jailed for seven years. Like several of his fellow Labour members at this time, he was later discovered to have been a communist spy.

Peter Baker

Combining the roles of publisher and politician (much like his associate Robert Maxwell), when Baker's business interests ran into trouble in 1954 he applied fake signatures to a number of letters before he was arrested and charged with seven counts of uttering forged documents. He pleaded guilty to six of these and received a sentence of seven years (later reduced to four). Incredibly, he remained an MP until after the case was decided, resigning only when he was finally incarcerated in Wormwood Scrubs.

Frank Russell, 2nd Earl Russell

A popular member of the House of Lords, Russell was nevertheless very much the black sheep of this distinguished political and philosophical dynasty. In 1901, he was famously tried for bigamy but sentenced to just three months in prison by a lenient judge on the grounds that at least one marriage had already caused him 'extreme torture'.

William Byron, 5th Baron Byron

In 1765, Lord Byron killed his cousin William Chaworth in a duel at a pub in Soho. He was tried for the crime but, under a statute dating back to the time of Edward VI, was found guilty only of manslaughter. Made to pay a modest fine, he nevertheless refused to express any regret for running his cousin through with a blade. Like Earl Russell, he thereafter revelled in his reputation as 'the wicked lord' and reportedly had his sword mounted and prominently displayed at Newstead Abbey.

David Chaytor

Caught up in the great Parliamentary expenses scandal of 2009, Labour backbencher Chaytor was the first to be hauled into court. After pleading guilty to a charge of false accounting, he was sentenced to eighteen months in prison. Others followed, although many appeared to escape with little more required of them than that they return to the public money they had seen fit to call their own.

Miranda Grell

After winning the Leyton ward of Waltham Forest for Labour by just twenty-eight votes, in September 2007 Grell went on trial under the Representation of the People

Act (1983). Charged with making a false allegation against a gay rival, specifically that he was a paedophile, she was fined £1,000 plus costs and barred from holding public office for three years.

The World's Most Famous Bell

At 6.00 p.m. each evening, the BBC broadcasts the chimes of Big Ben – live – on Radio 4. Bizarrely, anyone listening on the radio will hear the bongs before somebody standing at the foot of the tower, because the sound takes fractions of a second longer to travel down to the ground than through the ether.

For some reason, the hour bell is the only one to have a name – probably in memory of Sir Benjamin Hall, a generously proportioned Commissioner of Works – although the tower contains another four smaller bells.

With a diameter of 8 ft, and weighing in at 13.5 tons, Big Ben is the largest chiming[1] bell in the world and, after being cast at the Whitechapel Bell Foundry in April 1858, it took almost two weeks to cool down.

The bell tower itself leans slightly – by just over 8½ in. – to the northwest. It is not thought to be in any danger of falling down, although there was some concern about its stability during work on the Jubilee Line Extension in the 1990s.

The detailing on the much photographed clock faces at the top of the tower, each one a mammoth 23 ft in diameter, is by A. W. Pugin. All four feature the same Latin inscription: '*domine salvam fac reginam nostram victoriam primam*', meaning 'O Lord, keep safe our Queen Victoria the First'.

1 There's a much bigger bell in the Kremlin, weighing more than 200 tons, but it cracked before the Russians could use it and it has never been hung or sounded.

DISHONOURABLE MEMBERS (II)

TEN GREAT POLITICAL SEX SCANDALS

John Profumo

In 1963, Profumo's crime was lying to the House of Commons, but the likelihood is that his political career was doomed anyway. As Secretary of State for War, and a married man, he had no defence against press accusations that he was engaged in an improper relationship with a model.

At the height of the Cold War, his case gained added piquancy when it emerged that Christine Keeler was also seeing the Soviet Naval Attaché, Yevgeny Ivanov.

Involving sex and a spy, the resulting scandal holed the Macmillan Government below the waterline and it sank a few months later. Profumo wisely withdrew from public life and stayed hidden.

David Blunkett

Blunkett quit the Labour Cabinet in late 2004 following allegations that, as Home Secretary, he had fast-tracked a visa application for his lover's nanny. Worse still, besides being married to someone else, the lover in question was the publisher of the traditionally Tory-supporting *Spectator,* effectively the house journal of the British political right.

Any hopes in the Blair camp that further embarrassing revelations might die a death quickly evaporated; Blunkett, it seemed, was mounting a legal challenge. He did so to gain access to one of Kimberley Quinn's children on the grounds that he, rather than Mr Quinn, had fathered the two-year-old boy.

John Prescott

In April 2006, Deputy Prime Minister John Prescott (sixty-seven) admitted he had been having an extramarital affair with Tracey Temple (forty-three) who, at the time, worked for him as a secretary. The Member for Hull East said that the affair had ended 'some time ago' and that, of course, he regretted it.

Telling journalists, 'I have discussed this fully with my wife Pauline who is devastated,' he went on to say, 'I would be grateful if [we] can get on with our lives.' Mrs Prescott stood by him, only publishing her version of events a few years later in a book mawkishly entitled *Smile Though Your Heart Is Breaking*.

Jeremy Thorpe

The leader of the Liberal Party was driven out of office in 1976 after being forced to deny a homosexual relationship with sometime male model Norman Scott. Subsequently embroiled in an alleged conspiracy to kill Scott – the bungling hitman reportedly mistook Dunstable for Barnstaple – Thorpe was acquitted of all charges, but by that time his political career lay in ruins.

The dapper, Oxford-educated Old Etonian was a popular figure around Westminster and, by all accounts, a skilled politician. More than thirty years after the trial he has said little, beyond telling one reporter, 'If it happened now, I think the public would be kinder. Back then, they were very troubled by it.'

Robin Cook

Labour's Foreign Secretary from 1997 to 2001, Cook left his wife shortly after his appointment and following a telephone call from Tony Blair's Director of Communi cations. During the course of their conversation, Alastair Campbell warned Cook that the press had somehow got wind of his affair with Gaynor Regan, a member of his staff.

The two subsequently married, but not before Margaret Cook had gone on the record accusing Cook of being an insensitive husband and a secret alcoholic. She further alleged that the affair with Ms Regan was by no means his first but admitted after his death halfway up a mountain in 2005 that he had been an 'exemplary' father.

Paddy Ashdown

Politicians like to think they can keep a lid on things and, until the headlines started screaming 'PADDY PANTS-DOWN', the Lib-Dem leader might have assumed an affair with his secretary was nicely under wraps. But in 1992, Tricia Howard telephoned to warn him that one of the tabloids – the now defunct *News of the World* – had been in touch. By then the affair was over, but Ashdown admits that, on hearing this, 'I felt my stomach sink into a black pit'. Briefly, he considered taking out an injunction against the paper but, realising this would not work, he telephoned his wife before calling a press conference to confess to everything.

Anthony Lambton

Disclaiming the Earldom of Durham in order to remain in politics (but arrogantly insisting that he still be called 'Lord Lambton'), the MP for Berwick-upon-Tweed resigned in 1973 after his ignoble private life hit the headlines. In particular, the *News of the World* had evidence of numerous liaisons with prostitutes.

After the husband of one of the women had attempted to sell photographs of the member in action, the police swooped on Lambton's house and found a quantity of cannabis in the bedroom. With characteristic *hauteur*, Lambton claimed his debauchery was an attempt to soothe an aristocratic obsession, saying a previous attempt to cure himself by gardening had failed.

Iris Robinson

In late 2009 came news that the wife of the First Minister of the Northern Ireland Assembly – and a high-profile Democratic Unionist Party member herself – was withdrawing from public life. In the way of these things, the announcement came immediately after she'd been warned that a BBC documentary was due to broadcast details of her personal and financial affairs.

Earlier in the year, the couple, nicknamed 'the Swish Family Robinson', had been caught up in the MPs' expenses scandal following claims they were receiving £571,000 a year in salaries and expenses. It later emerged that Mrs Robinson, a controversially vocal, born-again Christian, had been having an affair with a teenager.

Cecil Parkinson

On the verge of being appointed to the post of Foreign Secretary, Parkinson was instead forced to resign from office in October 1983 when it became known that his former secretary, Sara Keays, was carrying his child. In 1987, he was politically rehabilitated by Lady Thatcher and made Secretary of State for Energy.

At the time of his disgrace, Parkinson claimed to have received many letters of support from the public. When Flora Keays turned eighteen, however, he took another pasting in the press when it was noted that he had never met his daughter and seemed to have no intention of doing so.

Jeffrey Archer

Britain's longest-running political sex scandal saw the fabled 'millionaire novelist' successfully suing a tabloid for saying he had paid for sex but then finding himself in the dock twelve years later accused of perverting the course of justice. Found guilty and forced to repay £500,000 damages, Archer was sentenced to four years in gaol.

As well as being expelled from the Conservative Party for five years (and the MCC for seven), the cricket-loving Archer had to stump up nearly £2 million once legal fees and interest were taken into account. Many of his friends stayed loyal, however, and his three volumes of prison diaries reportedly sold very well.

Parliamentary Figures of Speech

'It's in the bag'

Behind the Speaker's Chair is a large bag into which Members of Parliament drop petitions from constituents in the hope that these will be considered by the House. Obviously, MPs could still decide either way, or even ignore it, but the expression has come to mean that something is, wink-wink, sorted.

'Toeing the line'

Meaning to require someone to follow a certain course, this is popularly supposed to be a reference to a pair of parallel lines woven into the carpet of the debating chamber of the House of Commons. Opposing members must remain on their side of the relevant line, the two being positioned approximately two sword-lengths apart – plus an additional 6 in. to ensure nobody gets hurt in the cut and thrust. (In fact, members have always been forbidden to attend a session wearing a sword, and the hooks in the cloakrooms still include little ribbon loops designed to hold the swords of Members entering the Chamber.)

'Three-line whip'

Derived from eighteenth-century hunting practice when the whipper-in was responsible for driving stray hounds back into the pack. In political circles, 'taking the whip' implies membership of a party, and a commitment to adhere to its rules. To this end, voting instructions are issued to Members by the Whips' Office on slips of paper. A single underlining means attendance at a division is optional; a double underlining means it is compulsory unless the Member can pair off with a member of the Opposition (meaning neither will vote, thereby negating any advantage); and three underlinings means the member must vote and vote with his or her party – no matter what.

'Take a back seat'

Suggesting an individual will observe rather than taking an active role, the expression sounds like an automotive one but actually refers to his or her relocation from the front benches to the back ones.

'Economical with the actualité'

Just as MPs are forbidden to describe each other as liars, they have shown themselves, as a species, to be constitutionally unable to admit they have themselves uttered an untruth. In 1992, Alan Clark MP used this particular circumlocution to admit that he had actually done exactly that (when the veracity of some of his answers was more closely questioned) and his sly phrase has since entered the language.

'Tired and emotional'

Parliamentary rules also forbid one member from accusing another of being drunk, but it is considered acceptable to use one of several well-understood euphemisms. This one had its origins in the satirical weekly *Private Eye*, initially as reference to an apparently well-lubricated Labour Foreign Secretary of the 1960s. It has since caught on to such an extent that, in the opinion of many lawyers, it is itself now to be considered equally defamatory.

Please Don't Quote Me!

'It's nice to be in Cornwall again . . .'

Liberal Democrat Paddy Ashdown MP arriving in Devon for the 1992 General Election.

'How nice to see you all here!'

Roy Jenkins MP addressing a group of prisoners.

'Suicide is a real threat to health in this country.'

Conservative Minister Virginia Bottomley MP

'Headmasters of schools tend to be male.'

Labour MP Clare Short

'I am a working politician, not a thinker.'

Labour Home Secretary Jack Straw

'Everyone ought to be arrested at least once. It's an education.'

Conservative Alan Clark MP
after attempting to drive his Land Rover
through a police cordon.

'One reason I changed the Labour Party is so that we could remain true to our principles.'

Prime Minister Tony Blair

'Nobody would go to Hitler's funeral if he was alive today.'

Labour's Ron Brown MP

'The past is gone and is not coming back.'

Nick Clegg, Liberal Democrat Leader

'Clearly, the future is still to come.'

Peter Brooke MP

21

Ceremonial London

'Come with me, ladies and gentlemen, who are in any wise weary of London: come with me: and those that tire at all of the world we know: for we have new worlds here.'

Lord Dunsany (1905)

From Barnet to Whitehall, and from Beating Retreat to the Widow's Bun, London boasts scores of arcane customs and colourful ceremonies. Many date back hundreds of years but, as the following selection shows, they are still celebrated throughout in an annual calendar that is unmatched for symbolism, strangeness and variety by any city anywhere else in the world.

January

Royal Epiphany Gifts Ceremony

At St James's Palace on 6 January, a gift of gold, frankincense and myrrh is carried into the Chapel Royal by two Gentleman Ushers of the Royal Household while the scarlet-clad Gentlemen and Children of the Chapel Royal sing a Communion service. The valuable gifts (the gold is in the form of twenty-five sovereigns) are received by the Bishop of London in his role as Dean of the Chapel Royal, who bows three times in honour of the three wise men of the Nativity.

Charles I Commemoration

Marking the anniversary of the murder by execution of Charles I on 30 January 1649, members of the Royal Stuart Society hold services in several London churches on the last Sunday of the month. This is followed by a march by the King's Army – Royalist supporters in full Civil War regalia – to the place of his death, outside the Banqueting House on Whitehall.

February

Clown Service

In memory of clown prince Joseph Grimaldi (who lived at 56 Exmouth Market, Clerkenwell, from 1818 to 1828) a service is held on the last Sunday of February – or occasionally the first in March. The service takes place at Holy Trinity, Dalston, the official church of the International Clowns' Club, and costume and make-up are considered mandatory for those attending.

Farthing Bundles

Commemorating the Fern Street Settlement, an Edwardian charitable endeavour to alleviate poverty in the East End, the expression refers to parcels of newspaper containing small toys and oddments, which were given away to poor children small enough to pass under a ceremonial arch. Sadly, the practice has not been held regularly since the 1980s but the name of the instigator, Clara Grant, is commemorated in a building in Mellish Street, E14, and a little oak arch is occasionally erected in her memory.

Shrove Tuesday

Marked in Lincoln's Inn Fields by an annual pancake race, and at Westminster School with the celebrated Pancake Greaze. The latter sees a verger from the adjacent Abbey leading a procession of eager boys (and, since 1973, girls, too) out of the school where the cook tosses a huge pancake over a high bar. The competitors then race to grab a portion of the pancake; whoever secures the largest fragment receives a cash bonus from the Dean.

Blessing the Throats

On 3 February each year, at the pre-Reformation St Etheldreda's in Ely Place – London's oldest Catholic church – those stricken with illnesses of the throat seek a cure during a special service. Two long altar candles are blessed and crossed with ribbons, and, as supplicants kneel before the priest, he holds the Cross beneath their chins while intoning, 'May the Lord deliver you from the evil of the throat, and from every other evil.' The service commemorates the fourth-century St Blaise, an Armenian said to have saved a child from choking to death on the bone of a fish.

March

Widow's Bun

As described in Chapter 14 – Boozy London – this practice dates back at least two centuries and involves a sailor adding a hot cross bun every year to the collection hanging over the bar at the Widow's Son pub, Bromley-by Bow.

Graveside Dole

On Good Friday at Smithfield's St Bartholomew-the-Great, London's oldest church, it has long been the tradition to place twenty-one coins on a tomb in the church to be collected by a similar number of poor widows of the parish. In what is now a sparsely populated parish, and a relatively desirable and expensive place to live, poor widows are somewhat thinner on the ground. The service is still held, however, and the money used to buy hot cross buns for those children attending the service.

Sir John Cass Commemoration

Around the first week in March, staff, pupils and governors from the City's Sir John Cass Foundation schools mark their founder's life with a service at the church of St Botolph-without-Aldgate. A successful seventeenth-century merchant, alderman and MP, in 1710 Sir John established a school in the churchyard for the education of 50 boys and 40 girls, and 300 years later his foundation still supports an impressive variety of educational establishments in London. These include the Sir John Cass School of Art, London Metropolitan University, City University's Cass Business School, the University of East London and the Sir John Cass Redcoat School.

Oranges & Lemons Service

At the church of St Clement Danes in the Strand, one of the capital's newer traditions (it dates from the 1920s) sees children from local schools reading the lesson and, after reciting the famous rhyme – the tune of which is played on the church bells – receiving a gift of fruit from a pile outside the church door. It takes place on a weekday towards the end of March.

April

John Stow Commemoration

The life of the great historian and chronicler of the City of London is celebrated as near as possible to the anniversary of his death on 5 April 1605. Each year, the Lord Mayor of London replaces a quill in the stone hand of Stow's memorial in the church of St Andrew Undershaft in Leadenhall Street.

May

Oak Apple Day

In 1660, on 29 May, Charles II returned in triumph to London to the acclamation of his people and the sound of church bells ringing throughout the City. The Restoration of the Monarchy is marked on the anniversary each year, for example by Chelsea Pensioners who honour their founder by parading with oak sprigs recalling their sovereign's happy escape after hiding in an oak tree after his defeat at Worcester.

Florence Nightingale Commemoration

On or near the great lady's birthday (12 May), another, smaller group of Chelsea Pensioners, representing the wounded and dying of the Crimea, place a lamp on the High Altar of Westminster Abbey.

Swearing on the Horns

An oath to confirm the supplicant's commitment to drunkenness and debauchery, this Highgate peculiarity is of long standing but was clearly never more than a lively attempt to fleece eighteenth-century travellers making their way through the village en route to London. Twice a year, the tradition is celebrated at The

Wrestlers in North Road, with monies extracted from the participants being used to benefit local charities.

Samuel Pepys Commemoration

At his parish church and burial place – St Olave's, Hart Street – the life of London's celebrated diarist is marked each year, on a date as close as possible to the anniversary of his death on 26 May 1703. A wreath is laid on his tomb by the Lord Mayor, accompanied by music and songs that Pepys would have known.

June

Beating the Bounds

Walking and beating parish boundaries dates back at least as far as the eighth century, a ceremony intended to seek God's protection for crops, livestock and people. At All Hallows-by-the-Tower, the beating party comprises students of St Dunstan's College, Catford, who, with clergy and Liverymen, travel by boat each Ascension Day out to the middle of the Thames to mark the parish's southern boundary. Every three years, they stage a formal confrontation with the neighbouring parish (the Tower of London Liberty) as the two share a disputed boundary marker. In 1698, the participants actually rioted, but in modern times the Lord Mayor of London merely challenges the authority of the Resident Governor of the Tower.

Knollys Rose

One of the City's Quit Rent Ceremonies (see Odd Jobs, Chapter 13) in which symbolic rents are collected for certain lands or properties of antiquity in order to assert the overlord's ultimate title to that land. By agreement, such token rents may be paid in peppercorns (hence the phrase), red roses and even, in one celebrated case, a roast dinner.

The Knollys Rose is a reference to a famous fourteenth-century soldier, Sir Robert Knollys, and is made each year by the Verger of All Hallows-by-the-Tower in payment for a footbridge – now long gone – linking two properties believed once to have stood in Seething Lane. The ceremony takes place on Midsummer Day following a procession to the Mansion House, and the rent of a single red rose is paid in person to the Lord Mayor of London.

Bubble Sermon

A reminder to liverymen and freemen of the Worshipful Company of Stationers that 'life is but a bubble', the sermon is preached on the first Tuesday of June at St Martin's-within-Ludgate. This is done as per the will of one of the company's eighteenth-century benefactors, Richard Johnson.

July

Doggett's Coat & Badge

More venerable, longer and decidedly tougher than the Oxbridge affair, the world's oldest rowing race was conceived to mark the anniversary of George I's accession to the throne. It has been held each summer since 1715, and is supervised by the Fishmongers' Company, with only young members of the Worshipful Company of Watermen and Lightermen eligible to take part in the sculling challenge. The winner is presented with a scarlet coat and a large silver badge, having rowed $4^1/_2$ miles single-handedly while negotiating no fewer than ten bridges.

September

Oliver Cromwell Commemoration

On 3 September each year, the anniversary of the usurper's

victories at Dunbar and Worcester as well as of his own death in 1658, a short service is held by his statue outside Westminster Hall. Close to the date, the Roundhead Association, a sort of dour counterpart to the King's Army (see page 243), also musters a small force to march nearby, in memory of those who were hanged, drawn and quartered for killing their king.

October

Lion Sermon

On or about 16 October each year, at St Katherine Cree, Leadenhall Street, a sermon is preached at the behest of Sir John Gayer, a former Lord Mayor of London and a prime mover in the East India Company. Waylaid by a lion in the Arabian desert while on a trading mission, Sir John fell to his knees to pray and was saved. Since 1649, in his memory and on the anniversary of his escape, the service traditionally includes excerpts from the Book of Daniel.

Faggot Service

Another Quit Rent Ceremony (see page 247), the Faggot Service has been held every year for more than 800 years except during Cromwell's occupation. King John granted a piece of land at Eardington in Shropshire for a rent of two knives, one to be 'good enough to cut a hazel rod' and the other so bad that it would bend rather than cut 'green cheese'.

Today, the knives have been replaced by a hatchet and a billhook, but, in order to prove that the debt is discharged, a ceremony at the Law Courts in the Strand each year sees the Solicitor of the City of London – on the order of the Queen's Remembrancer – demonstrating that one blade cannot cut a hazel rod before using a second to break a faggot or bundle of them into pieces.

Harvest of the Sea Service

A piscatorial variation on a traditional school or church harvest festival, mid-October sees workers from Billingsgate Fish Market – now removed to the Isle of Dogs – making their annual pilgrimage to their former parish church, St Mary-at-Hill, for a service of thanksgiving. The occasion is marked by an unusually fine display of fish on a marble slab in the church porch – traditionally thirty-nine species were put on display, an echo of the Church of England's Thirty-Nine Articles – the produce being afterwards distributed to those in need.

November

Lord Mayor of London's Installation

The most magnificent piece of civil ceremonial in the country relates to a particularly ancient office and one that, after more than 800 years, still vests in a single person not just the office of Lord Mayor of London but also that of Chief Magistrate of the City, Admiral of the Port of London, Chancellor of City University, President of Gresham College and President of the City of London Reserve Forces.

Granted the precedence of an earl, made a member of the Privy Council and privileged to travel abroad without a passport, the incumbent also gets to live at the Mansion House, albeit for one year only, before being knighted by his sovereign. (If the incumbent is a woman, incidentally, she is still known as Lord Mayor and never as the Lady Mayoress.)

The election of a new Lord Mayor will already have taken place on Michaelmas Day at Guildhall, the oldest secular building in the capital. This is symbolically barricaded on the day with a wooden structure called the Wickets put in place and uniformed beadles installed to ensure that none but liverymen get to cast a vote.

Just as the voters are limited – somewhat surprisingly for such an important post – so, too, are the candidates, who must both be senior aldermen of the city and have served a term as sheriff. Of the two, the more senior is always chosen, which is to say that each year the result is already a foregone conclusion. The procedure is nevertheless a deeply solemn one, with as much colour and pageantry as a papal conclave – and the same strict sense of time-honoured formality.

The celebrations have to wait a few weeks more, however, when the new Lord Mayor is finally installed as the City's new 'chief citizen'. Expressly more public than the covert deliberations of the liverymen, this involves the new incumbent heading a lengthy, noisy and colourful procession more than 3½ miles long. It is a spectacle that attracts hundreds of thousands of spectators each year, as the new lord's eighteenth-century gold carriage makes its way from the City of London to the City of Westminster where an oath of loyalty is sworn to the Crown.

After 500 years, the Lord Mayor's Show is still the oldest, longest and most popular such procession anywhere in the world, and – rain or shine – it takes place on the second Saturday in November.

December

Trafalgar Square Christmas Tree

Presented to the people of London every year since 1947, the tree 'is given by the city of Oslo as a token of Norwegian gratitude to the people of London for their assistance during the years 1940–45'.

It is decorated in a traditional Nordic fashion, and supplemented by 500 white bulbs, which are lit on the second Thursday of the month. This is done in the presence of the Lord Mayor of Westminster, musicians and carol singers from

St Martin-in-the-Fields, and many thousands of members of the public. For retailers, Christmas may have started back in October, but for many Londoners this is the true sign.

22

Esoteric London

London's Arcane and Secret Societies

'Secret' doesn't necessarily have to mean 'sinister', but there's nothing quite like excluding everyone else to get the collective imagination racing and conspiracy theorists jumping up and down.

After more than 300 years, London's traditional gentlemen's clubs, for example, continue to arouse suspicion and resentment in equal measure, even though little happens inside most of them that you wouldn't find at any suburban golf club.

The Freemasons have similarly been pilloried for centuries for their apparent obsession with keeping things under wraps, so much so that many non-Masons seem to believe that their decision to throw open the doors of their Covent Garden HQ – anyone can turn up at Great Queen Street for a guided tour – is actually some kind of a double bluff and that really the movement is headquartered somewhere else altogether.

The truth, however, is probably just that the average member of this sort of place just wants somewhere to have a quiet drink and a chat with like-minded chaps – and, yes, even now, it is nearly always chaps rather than chapesses who tend to make up the membership.

Calves' Head Club

Established to meet at premises in Suffolk Street on 30 January each year to celebrate the murder of Charles I, the society survived into the eighteenth century but is now thought to be defunct. The name derived from the dishes served, a reference presumably to the removal of the king's own head.

In the 1730s, the event got so out of hand that troops were called, and today those with Cromwellian leaning are more likely to join the aforementioned Roundhead Association and their annual march in Whitehall each autumn.

City of Lushington

A somewhat elaborate drinking club – the name comes from 'lush' – the society was founded in Great Russell Street in the 1760s and was still active in the area a century and a half later. Chiefly comprising 'theatricals, singers, literary men, jovial tradesmen and well-to-do mechanics' – i.e. pretty much anyone – the members would drink themselves silly under the watchful eye of a president dressed as the Lord Mayor with four 'Aldermen' on hand to ensure that newly elected candidates stood their rounds.

The Club

TV news anchor Jeremy Paxman stumbled by accident upon The Club in the 1990s while researching his book *Friends in High Places: Who Runs Britain?* A member carelessly described it to him as 'the Establishment at play' before realising (a) that Paxo had never heard of it and (b) that he had thus inadvertently helped quite a big cat out of its bag.

It is super-exclusive – Lord Chancellors and senior bishops are among those who have been blackballed during its 250-year history – and it comprises barely fifty individuals, all of them male. Mostly senior politicians, academics, financiers and members of the Great and Good, they still meet for dinner one Tuesday each month in a private dining room at 60 St James's Street.

Freemasons

The archetypal secret society, Freemasons also make up the largest such group in London. Their origins are genuinely ancient – enabling medieval stone masons to move around the country to find work – but the society became much bigger much later.

The oldest Lodge in London is thought to date back to 1691, and, while members typically meet in fairly conventional buildings, the capital boasts a number of quite stupendous temples. These include an especially lavish one hidden somewhat unexpectedly behind locked doors in the former Great Eastern Hotel by Liverpool Street Station. Designed by Charles Barry Jr. (at a cost equivalent to £4 million today), it is not open to the public but can be hired for weddings.

Golden Dawn

The Hermetic Order of the Golden Dawn was established in London in the nineteenth century, its members engaging in theurgy or the practice of summoning a god or gods into being. Possibly they still do, as the organisation has a website, but this is noticeably unhelpful, declaring simply that 'the London Temple Chiefs have decided that there will be no information about, or reference to, the temple or the order'.

Gormogons

The Ancient, August and Noble Order of Gormogons announced themselves to the public in a newspaper advertisement in London's *Daily Post* on 3 September 1724. The founder Philip Wharton had been expelled from the Freemasons, and consequently made it a rule that no Mason could join his new order without first burning his regalia and agreeing to be ridiculed. Unsurprisingly, few found the restrictions appealing and, by 1738, the organisation seems to have disappeared.

The Hellfire Club

Perhaps the best known of the eighteenth-century secret societies, the so-called Mad Monks of Medmenham, a group of allegedly wild and dissipated aristocrats, famously gathered at the Buckinghamshire abbey of that name to celebrate black Masses while performing acts of 'gross lewdness and daring impiety' on the ruined altar.

Afterwards, it was said, they would eat strange foodstuffs served by naked girls on whom they liked to press their basest desires. However, much of this stuff is now thought to have been made up, as the club's origins were solidly London-based and, as early meetings were held at the George & Vulture in the City, it seems unlikely that the landlord would have been entirely happy to see his barmaids used in this way.

The Oddfellows

Rudely described as a kind of cut-price Freemasons, this fraternal society is sometimes said to have been established by a group of knights in the 1450s, although a foundation date of around 1745 seems more likely.

Documents exist showing that, at that time, members were

paying a penny to attend meetings at Southwark's Oakley Arms, the Globe at Hatton Garden and the Boar's Head in Smithfield, and concerned themselves mostly with self-help and companionship. Over the years, the membership in London included George IV, Winston Churchill and Stanley Baldwin, with the fathers of George Harrison and Ringo Starr joining one of the provincial fraternities.

The Order of Chaeronea

Taking its name from a fourth-century battle between a Macedonian king and the Sacred Band of Thebes (who lost), the Order was founded in the 1890s by the poet G. C. Ives as a sort of underground network for gay men. New members were required to swear 'never to vex or persecute lovers' and 'that all real love shall be to you as sanctuary'.

To his lasting disappointment, Ives was unable to persuade his friend Oscar Wilde to join his fellow members, who adopted a wide range of arcane and esoteric codewords and symbols. Almost certainly they did this because at this time – as Wilde's own experience was soon to demonstrate – the penalties for being found out were decidedly extreme.

The Theosophical Society

From the Greek *theos* (god) and *sophia* (wisdom), the Society was founded in 1875 by Helena Blavatsky in New York and was active in London within two or three years. Writers seemed particularly attracted to it, and several names appear in its history including Sir Arthur Conan Doyle, W. B. Yeats, Lewis Carroll and Sir Henry Rider Haggard.

Still active today (in Gloucester Place, W1), it welcomes students of all religions and none; indeed, anyone keen to 'form a nucleus of the universal brotherhood of humanity, to encourage the study of comparative religion, philosophy and science, and to investigate the unexplained laws of nature and the powers latent in man'.

The 33rd Degree

Despite a brass plaque on the wall at 10 Duke Street, London, SW1, boldly identifying the building as the Headquarters of the Supreme Council of the 33rd Degree, it took until 1984 and the publication of Stephen Knight's book *The Brotherhood* to alert the wider public to the existence of the very highest echelons of the Masonic movement.

Knight even went so far as to suggest in his book that the organisation was so secret that even most Freemasons did not realise that there were more than three degrees or levels to their craft. The truth, he said, was that there were actually another thirty levels and that, headed by a 'Most Puissant Sovereign Commander', only seventy-five Masons could attain the ultra-exclusive 33rd Degree at any one time.

Wolf Club

The nineteenth-century actor Edmund Kean was once charged with having a criminal conversation, a wonderful euphemism for an adulterous affair. He also found time to establish a club-within-a-pub at the Coal Hole on the Strand, so-named as it was popular with colliers working the Thames.

Kean and his fellow members like to claim they were henpecked husbands, innocents who were forbidden by their wives to sing in the bath, but more likely is that they came here to get drunk and to mix with the kind of women no wife ever wants to hear about.